LEADERSHIP CHRONICLES

LEADERSHIP CHRONICLES

DEBASHIS CHATTERJEE

**PENGUIN
BUSINESS**

An imprint of Penguin Random House

PENGUIN BUSINESS

USA | Canada | UK | Ireland | Australia
New Zealand | India | South Africa | China | Singapore

Penguin Business is part of the Penguin Random House group of companies
whose addresses can be found at global.penguinrandomhouse.com

Published by Penguin Random House India Pvt. Ltd
4th Floor, Capital Tower 1, MG Road,
Gurugram 122 002, Haryana, India

Penguin
Random House
India

First published in Penguin Business by Penguin Random House India 2023

10 9 8 7

ISBN 9780670098651

Typeset in Adobe Garamond Pro by Manipal Technologies Limited, Manipal
Printed at Replika Press Pvt. Ltd, India

www.penguin.co.in

MIX
Paper | Supporting
responsible forestry
FSC™ C016779

To Aditi,
co-creator of the most memorable moments
of my life's chronicles

Contents

Contents

Foreword

Learning from Everyday Life Makes One a Leader

A book on leadership doesn't have to focus solely on leaders in the conventional sense. A leader's traits are best understood by examining those they followed because a good leader is also a good follower. Debashis has been inspired by intriguing leaders throughout his life, but he hasn't copied their styles. Instead, he remains original while drawing inspiration from figures like his grandmother, a window cleaner or a world-famous professor who prefers shouldering his luggage.

I have known Debashis for about three decades. His multiple initiatives at Indian Institute of Management Kozhikode (IIMK) have seemingly created many new benchmarks. IIMK had one of the highest proportions of female students a decade ago when other IIMs only had 15–20 per cent. During my visit to the institute, I saw the indelible impact of Debashis' thoughts on the campus as a whole. Inspiring quotes welcome the visitor creating an optimistic mood. He also pioneered the first MBA in liberal studies in India. I co-taught a course on Gandhian leadership that Debashis designed for this programme. I also had the honour of speaking at the Globalizing Indian Thought Conclave which has now become an annual feature at IIMK. Leadership is to do what you believe in without looking for precedence.

Just like ants following a trail, Debashis didn't actively search for opportunities; they naturally came his way, as they do for everyone. Some people seize those opportunities, learning from even the smallest oddities, while others let them slip away. The age-old question of whether leaders are born or made, influenced by nature or nurture, remains intriguing, but we won't delve into that debate here. Instead, I hope that, as readers of this book encounter these delicately described moments, they may find a spark igniting within them, reinforcing my point.

This book highlights how inadequacies, which we all suffer from, can be a source of our strength, sometimes serendipitously but sometimes, by what you make of them. Having got second division in higher secondary school exams mainly because of just passing marks in English and drawing, I fully understand what an education in vernacular language could mean for a young mind. I admire the tenacity, fortitude and a bit of idiosyncrasy which paved the way on which this story has been enacted. The pebbles along the way will stand as testimony to the fact that it has not been easy. However, it has been very meaningful. Breaking the sixty-year tradition of ABC (Ahmedabad-Bangalore-Calcutta, the top three IIMs) by IIMK to turn it into ABK is not a small achievement. David is alive and kicking. Beware, the Goliaths of the world!

—Anil Gupta
former professor of IIM Ahmedabad,
founder of Honey Bee Network,
fellow of the World Academy of Arts and Sciences

Introduction

The Rise of a Star

द्वा सुपर्णा सयुजा सखाया समानं वृक्षं परिषस्वजाते ।
तयोरन्यः पिप्पलं स्वाद्वत्त्यनश्रन्नन्यो अभिचाकशीति ॥ १ ॥

Mundaka Upanishad, chapter 3, canto 1, verse 1

The quoted verse means, 'Two birds, inseparable companions, perch on the same tree. One eats the fruit on the tree; the other looks on without eating.'

The first bird is the individual self, feeding on the pleasures and pains of this world; the other is the observer self, silently witnessing it all.

Fixing his gaze on the treetop outside his glass-panelled office, the 'Prime Mover' says, 'Leadership is more about observation than action. A bias for action, as in the Hollywood model of the leader as a hero on horseback, completely overshadows the power of the astute observer behind the impactful actor . . . I am simply a learner, and I teach because I need to learn better.'

This simple, matter-of-fact description of Professor Debashis' role is at the heart of his pioneering work as a teacher and institution-builder.

I have been following Prof. Debashis Chatterjee's writings for over two decades. I continue to be fascinated and enriched by how he has quietly and significantly altered the understanding of leadership from the vantage point of the wisdom traditions of India.

Debashis is not just a writer, academic or institution builder. I think he is one of the great thinkers of our time. I have seen him evolve from a professor and institution builder to a global thought leader. As lieutenant governor of Puducherry, I invited him to the Raj Nivas to talk to my senior administrators. The clarity and deep understanding that he brought to us that day left all of us mesmerized. Later, he released my biographical work along with Indra Nooyi. I recall how Indra invited Debashis to speak first, out of respect, about his work.

Over the years, I have had the opportunity to visit him on the IIM Kozhikode campus. I have seen the impact of his transformative vision in building a world-class institution. I am grateful to be able to share here my first-hand experience of seeing him at work.

Professor Debashis Chatterjee's eloquence has helped people comprehend the depth of these lines from the Mundaka Upanishad. Debashis, whom a colleague described as a 'Prime Mover', lives by the maxim, 'Leadership is a synthesis of reflection and action. Reflection is the software and action is the hardware of leadership.' He believes that the most valuable outcome of education is the development of a competent and compassionate human being. Self-effacing, sharp and with a keen eye for detail, he is popularly known as a 'leadership guru' among those who have been awed by the profundity of his thoughts, words and actions.

Debashis has roots in a small town in Bengal. His knowledge and insights made him traverse the globe. On his journeys, his persona touched the lives of innumerable people, motivated many and transformed many more. Every person who has been a part of his journey, in whatever way, has experienced the transformational touch of his presence. Debashis, who visited Harvard University twice as a Fulbright Scholar, completed thirty years of national service in four IIMs across the country where he has played leadership roles: director of the Indian Institute of Management, Kozhikode, for three terms spanning two decades; co-convenor of the Management Centre for Human Values, IIM Calcutta; dean of IIM Lucknow; mentor-director of IIM Amritsar; dean of S.P. Jain Global School, Singapore; and director-general at the International Management Institute, Delhi. The growth witnessed by all these institutes has been enormous under his able stewardship. His ceaseless efforts and untiring aspirations have left global imprints. When it comes to Indian education, he is one of the handful of people who know a lot about how it works.

This book is a narrative woven around his work and line of thought to commemorate the silver jubilee of IIM Kozhikode and his thirty years of excellence in teaching, writing and institutional leadership. Debashis has become increasingly well known worldwide as a teacher, author, thought leader and trailblazer in building institutions. This book is a humble attempt to understand the narrative of the journey of a stalwart who believes that education of the heart will be critical in a world of profound interconnectedness. He says that *Buddhivritti* (head) and *Hridayavritti* (heart) must work together to develop the self, others and larger systems.

This is a narrative about the disposition of a nationally acclaimed professor, his work, style, orientation, beliefs, principles, choices, and everything that he is and stands for. His style of writing adds a unique flavour to this body of work. His thoughts about his life as an insider and about the people who have been connected with him are intricately woven into this book.

While Debashis talks about the important phases of institution building in the different workplaces in his career, he also delves into how the path-breaking initiatives taken by him have made all the difference at these places. He openly shares insights from his personal and professional journeys, and sheds light on how his endeavours transformed institutions and people's lives. The perspectives, stories, insights, anecdotes and thoughts shared by his professional associates, friends, students and family members about him add an intriguing flavour to this narrative, making it a blend of the why, how, what and who of his unique work.

This book also explores Debashis' leadership philosophy— beginning with breaking the biases around the idea of globalizing Indian thought—and how it worked well in the organizations he transformed. His effort will inspire future generations of teachers, leaders and institution-builders to take his legacy to greater heights.

This book is set in twelve illuminating chapters, catering to different phases of his journey of transformative ideas. These ideas are best described as 'moving molecules in the mind'. Each chapter is a peek into an extra dimension of his trip. It is a blend of finely woven chronicles, meaningful responses to questions he has confronted and the world's testimonials about him. The reader is about to delve into a voyage of learning, interpreting and applying life lessons from a ringside view of a maverick teacher's life.

With reverence,

Dr Kiran Bedi

1

Moments of Life
That Refuse to Be Ordinary

Memories make our lives meaningful, giving consistency to the inconsistent events in them. I have often found it difficult to keep pace with my own life. My professional career of three decades just sprinted by. It is funny how one cannot keep oneself in step in the crazy race that is one's own life. That's how it was for me. My professional career zoomed by like a Ferrari on a highway, and my memory of it is more like that of a kid on a bicycle, pedalling frantically just to keep up.

So, life whizzed by at breakneck speed. But the story of it? Now . . . that's something special. I understand today that you are not defined by the actual experiences of your life but by the story of your life that you choose to remember. And, though my life did fly by like a supersonic jet, leaving behind what I thought was a blur of images and incidents, upon jogging my memory, I did find a lot of intact pictures in it. Those are what I have stitched together into this book.

Let's face it—writing a memoir is like doing one's laundry. You hang all your washed clothes out on the line and let them flap in the breeze. Some of them are bright and flashy, like a neon green T-shirt or a pair of purple pyjamas. Others are more boring, like plain old white socks or underwear that has seen better days. But, just as with your laundry, you've got to be careful about what you air out in public. You don't want to offend anyone's delicate sensibilities or reveal too much about yourself, you know. So, you've got to pick and choose what you share, and maybe toss a little fabric softener in there for good measure.

I am my own storyteller. Having led institutions for over two decades, I have come to appreciate the power of stories. A simple story well told can have a greater impact than tonnes of theories.

Through stories, leaders can communicate their vision, values and priorities to their team. Stories can be so inspiring that they can make a real difference in the culture and performance of individuals and institutions.

The stories I am about to tell you are of those fleeting but momentous events that defined and illuminated my life. So, here goes!

Why my grandmother refused to eat mangoes

The one defining feature of leadership is unselfishness. If there is one human trait that repels most people, it is selfishness. You cannot be a leader unless you have followers. Who follows a selfish man or woman to the ends of the world? Perhaps no one.

The woman from whom I learnt my first lessons in leadership was my grandmother. She was known as Sabasona. She had sharp features and a golden complexion, like an Alfonso mango.

Now, let me tell you, this woman loved mangoes. She loved them the way a kid loves a birthday cake. But she never had a single one herself. Nope. At least, for the years of my memory of her. She sliced them up with the precision of a surgeon and gave them all away to anyone who would take them. And when I asked her why she never kept any for herself, she just gave me this toothless smile that said more than words ever could.

But one day, when I was a little older, she let me in on her secret. It turned out that my grandfather, whom she loved more than anything and anybody else in the world, used to share their home-grown mangoes with her. And when he passed away, she just couldn't bring herself to eat them anymore. It was as if every mango was now a reminder of him, and she couldn't bear to enjoy it without him.

This woman's story touched my heart deeply, revealing a true hero and leader in every aspect. Her remarkable example taught me that leadership goes far beyond authority and power; it revolves around selflessness and creating a positive impact on the lives of others. Her unwavering dedication to hospitality reflected that. Whenever unexpected guests arrived, even at odd hours, she would spring into action, tirelessly preparing a meal for them. Her rest and leisure took a backseat as she devoted herself to meeting the needs of her visitors. It was as if their comfort and happiness became her sole mission, and she spared no effort in ensuring they felt welcome and cared for.

But it wasn't just strangers who experienced her hospitality. She also showcased her incredible patience and understanding in navigating the intricacies of our joint family. Within the household, each member had their quirks, interests and preferences that could easily lead to conflicts. Yet, she effortlessly embraced the diverse shades of personalities and catered to the unique needs of every family member.

She knew that true harmony stemmed from embracing differences rather than trying to mould everyone into one shape. With grace, she accommodated the varying interests and idiosyncrasies, creating an atmosphere of acceptance and love within the family.

When she passed away, the entire village came to her home to pay their respects. This woman, who preferred to live by herself, and who only had her immediate family for company, had touched so many lives with her kindness and generosity. The turnout of men, women and children with tearful eyes that day was a testament to the power of unselfishness, and a lesson that I'll never forget. Rest in peace, Sabasona. And enjoy all the mangoes you want, wherever you are up there.

So, how does unselfishness help in laying the foundation of leadership? Unselfishness teaches you to become sensitive to what you may call 'the other-oriented universe'. You learn to see reality beyond yourself and your wants and desires.

Now, you might still be thinking, 'How does this other-centred universe connect with leadership?' And to that, my friend, I must say: in every way. Unselfishness is the secret sauce to making a good leader great. It teaches you to open your eyes and see the world beyond your little bubble of self-centeredness. Suddenly, you're sensitive to the needs and wants of others, and that's a big part of what makes a leader truly effective.

Here's the kicker: when you start thinking beyond yourself, you discover a whole new world of possibilities. A world that's rich with potential and opportunity. And that's when authentic leaders are born. They don't get bogged down by their ego and limitations. They're able to see the bigger picture and take advantage of all the opportunities that are out there waiting for them.

So, yes. Unselfishness is kind of a big deal when it comes to leadership. It's the key to expanding your personal and professional identities, and it's what sets great leaders apart from the rest. If you want to be a leader that people look up to and respect, start thinking beyond yourself and see what kind of magic you can make happen. The limiting idea that confines your sense of self within your skin will broaden to encompass the selves of others.

As a result, your personal and professional identities will expand. You will discover a world beyond your ego. An ego-less world, rich with possibilities.

How I succeeded in spelling 'circus'

I owe much of my personal and professional success to a series of fortuitous circumstances. I can say I was, to an extent, lucky. The intensity of effort, amplified by a little luck, brings success. One such instance involved gaining admission to the prestigious St Xavier's School in my home town.

At the time, I was a student in class four at the local Town School in Bardhaman (then called Burdwan), where we were treated more like furniture than like students. The headmaster communicated more through his cane than words, and I lived in constant fear of being caught with uncombed hair or untrimmed nails. Learning was largely done by rote, and I endured the agonizing sounds of my classmates reciting poems and multiplication tables like croaking frogs. The only reprieve was the lush green football field that I could see through the iron bars of the classroom window. I longed for a school without classrooms.

St Xavier's School represented a space of aspiration. The students rode in school buses that navigated the narrow roads and alleys of Bardhaman town with a confident swagger, and they read Tintin comic books. I knew this because my younger brother had been admitted to the same school. The fees at St Xavier's were much higher than at Town School, and my father, a railway employee, could only afford to send one of us to St Xavier's.

One morning, I mustered up the courage to ask my father if I could also attend St Xavier's. My father, who loved me unconditionally, didn't say much at the time. Later, I learned that he had mortgaged a piece of land so he could afford to pay the tuition fees for both his children in the only English-medium school in town.

When I took the admission test at St Xavier's, reality hit me hard. Brother Murphy, a native of Australia, administered a spelling test, and I misspelt all 100 words on the test. The next day, my answer sheet, covered in red Xs, was displayed on the notice board outside the headmaster's office. Any other father would have been ashamed of his son, but mine was determined to get me into the school. He asked Father Hinque from Belgium to allow me to retake the test in a month. 'He's an intelligent boy,' my father pleaded. 'He's just not accustomed to hearing Australian English. Give him another chance.'

Father Hinque, the Belgian headmaster, reluctantly agreed; my father says he nodded his head up and down and from side to side as if to say, 'You can try, but your son will never make it.' My father struck a deal with the husband of the English teacher at St Xavier's to coach me for the spelling test. The underlying assumption was that he would 'leak the questions' so that I wouldn't fail again.

But Mr S.K. Saxena, the tutor and husband of the English teacher, Aparajita Saxena, had a reputation to uphold. He couldn't help but admit someone who had scored zero out of 100 on a spelling test to his roster of students who were weak in English. So, he administered another spelling test to all of the students, including me. 'Boys, can you spell circus for me?' he asked, in his acquired British accent. All of the other boys fumbled, but I confidently shouted out, 'C-I-R-C-U-S!'

'Excellent!' Saxena exclaimed. 'Admitted! Look at this boy who studied at the one-rupee-seventy-five-paise-per-month Town School and still managed to spell "circus" correctly. He will go very far!' My imagination ran wild. It was not that I was any better than those who had failed the test, but when I rode my bicycle to my tuition class, I had seen a massive billboard advertising the GEMINI CIRCUS that had come to town. The word 'CIRCUS' was printed in bold, colourful lettering inside the mouth of a hippopotamus.

I started my journey at St Xavier's without the benefit of a leaked paper, determined to master the English language. I fumbled, faltered and was made fun of. One learned that leadership could come from both aspiration and desperation. Aspiration can align one's thoughts and emotions, as a magnet does iron filings, while desperation can act like a fire that someone has set off in your hair. Both can mobilize human energy in extraordinary ways.

Now, after seventeen books, written in English, I still have nightmares about failing an English language test. But I know that my success in spelling 'circus' was more than just luck. It was a combination of aspiration and desperation, visual learning and a determination to succeed. To that unknown artist who had painted the word 'circus' inside the mouth of a hippo, I am grateful.

Meeting Tenzing, the first man to climb Mount Everest

Tenzing Norgay, a Sherpa who by conventional standards appears to be an unremarkable man, was my hero in school. During my visit to the Himalayan Mountaineering Institute in Darjeeling, when I was in fifth grade, I met a man cleaning a window with a mop. He asked what I wanted, and I replied, with an air of self-importance, that I wanted Tenzing's autograph.

'You have an autograph book?' he asked, in a botched accent.

'No, but I have a currency note,' I said.

'You have a pen?' he asked.

'Sorry, I don't have one with me,' I replied.

'I'll get one,' he said and moved towards a table.

'Where is Tenzing?' I asked, barely hiding my excitement as I scanned the hall to spot the great man.

The crazy man parked his mop on the window sill and signed my currency note.

'Not yours,' I cried. 'I want Tenzing's autograph.'

The man's expressionless face broke into a sheepish smile as he said, 'Tenzing is me!'

I watched in wonder as he signed my green five-rupee currency note with a flourish. Even as a young kid, I could sense what it meant for someone to achieve the extraordinary feat of being the first man to climb Mount Everest. It was a lesson in humility.

Armed with Tenzing's autograph, I came downhill from the Himalayan Mountaineering Institute, thinking of Tenzing's partner Edmund Hillary's words on mountain climbing: 'It is not the mountain that we conquer but ourselves.'

When leaders see a mountain out there, whether in the form of a challenge or a difficult problem, it triggers inner growth. The mountain generates willpower within. Wherever there is a wall blocking one's path, there is a corresponding mental will within everyone that can be summoned to surmount that block.

The triumph of 'will over the wall' is what we often describe as leadership.

Decoding the secret of a half-boiled egg

My first visit to the United States as a Rotary International exchange fellow in the nineties was an eye-opener. I saw a rich country and generous people. In those years, India was still coming to terms with a more liberalized economy, whereas the United States was the sole superpower, dizzy with 'affluenza' and military might.

In India, you had an aspiring middle class and a despairing poverty-stricken population struggling to make ends meet and still going to bed hungry. Indian roads, like the Indian economy, were still works in progress. Whereas in most developed countries you drove keeping either to the right or left, in India, you drove on whatever was left of the roads!

As part of my exchange programme, I spoke before a large audience in New Hampshire, on the east coast of the US. The theme of my talk was the India of those times. It was the India of the 1900s.

I asked an eager audience, 'What does a half-boiled egg mean to you?'

There were murmurs and some raised eyebrows in the audience.

An elderly American gentleman responded: 'Why, an egg boiled for half the usual time!'

I said, 'In my growing-up years in India, a half-boiled egg meant a fully boiled egg cut in two near-equal halves by a fine cotton string.'

My audience seemed startled.

I went on to explain further, 'That is how my mother used to cut an egg so that the two of us, my brother and I, could share an egg for our school tiffin. One whole egg was a luxury even for a growing kid.'

There was a hushed silence in the room.

Human motivation, I said, was about two simultaneous questions that humans often have to ask:

The first: how much more do I need to be happy?

And the second: how much less can I have and still be equally happy?

Whenever I trudged along the broken roads of Kolkata (then Calcutta) paved with pain and poverty, it was the second question that I was always reminded of.

Leaders learn to be more resourceful than others. They find opportunities in problems. They learn to make do with scarce resources to produce stunning results. You can think of Mahatma Gandhi or Nelson Mandela or even those Silicon Valley pioneers who inherited no legacy or large resources and yet were most resourceful.

Leader: Born or made? Insights from Lee Kuan Yew, architect of Singapore

Are leaders born, or made?

I once stumbled upon a classic nature-versus-nurture debate at Harvard, over whether people are born leaders, innately in possession of the necessary qualities, or whether they can be made so through training and experience. And when the sparring partners are a Harvard professor at one end and the architect of modern Singapore at the other, one is all ears. I was witness to this debate during my post-doctoral Fulbright fellowship at Harvard's Kennedy School of Government. I had just heard Lee Kuan Yew's inspiring talk on the rise of modern Singapore, and it was during the Q&A session following this that Professor Howard Gardner fired off his question. And Yew did not disappoint with his answer.

'Leaders can be made provided they are born,' he said, with a sly grin. The hall erupted in laughter. But, as Professor Gardner's furrowed brow indicated, this was no joking matter. Gardner wasn't amused. He wanted to hear more.

Lee Kuan Yew went on to explain his perspective on leadership, likening leadership fostering to the art of training sheepdogs in Australia. Apparently, you can spot an alpha dog by the intensity in its eyes—that's the dog born to lead. And just the way you can't train a non-alpha dog to have that kind of intensity, you can't train a person to be a leader unless he or she has the innate qualities that make for a leader.

That kind of reasoning hits me right in the gut. As someone who's always fancied himself a bit of a leader, it was a little disheartening to think that maybe it's all out of one's control. But at the same time, it's kind of freeing. If you are born with the stuff leaders are made of, then that's just who you are. And if you're not, well, that's okay too. There are plenty of other important roles to play in this world.

It was a simple yet profound analogy from Yew that went straight to my heart. I looked at some of the qualities I was born with and came to the conclusion: you may as much choose to be a leader as you would choose your parents.

But I still wondered—are some people born with the innate ability to lead, or can anyone become a leader, given the right training?

How John Naisbitt gave me a frame for the future

Picture it: Harvard Square, 2002. I was a nobody among a group of somebodies. I felt a lot like a kid with a sweet tooth who had to choose between fifteen different varieties of ice cream. I was invited by Professor John Kotter of Harvard Business School to be part of a leadership conclave with fourteen other thought leaders from across the world. My name was recommended for this thought leadership summit by the renowned management guru, Peter M. Senge of MIT's Sloan School.

I was overwhelmed to be among an intimidating cast of characters. They were some of the best minds of the world: Gary

Hamel, Nitin Nohria, Sally Helgesen, Charles Handy, Margaret J. Wheatley, Peter Senge . . . then there was also John Naisbitt, an adviser to US presidents. Naisbitt was a celebrity author and public speaker in the area of future studies. His first book, *Megatrends: Ten New Directions Transforming Our Lives*, the result of almost ten years of research, was published in 1982 and was on the *New York Times* bestseller list for two years, mostly as no. 1. It was published in fifty-seven countries and sold more than fourteen million copies. John Naisbitt had been the recipient of fifteen honorary doctorates in the humanities, technology and science.

Naisbitt invited me to visit him at his home near Harvard Square. You can imagine the thoughts that raced through my mind when Naisbitt himself lifted my heavy suitcase as I entered his home. It was not just humbling but also truly enlightening to see this embodiment of that ancient Indian phrase, *vidya dadati vinayam,* true knowledge begets humility.

Naisbitt's writing room was a large, whitewashed hall; there were plenty of newspaper clippings pasted here and there and notes written on multi-coloured sticky pads. Naisbitt told me that he had been spotting trends for ten years by scanning the newspapers and tapping into other sources. 'My wife gave up on me because I was obsessed with data and trends, and I married my literary agent when we got divorced,' he told me. I was beginning to feel sorry for him. Naisbitt took me in his stride explaining that big ideas do matter in academic life.

But what really struck me was Naisbitt's parting advice to me: 'You have to have a solid framework inside your head to be able to predict the future. A mental framework helps you see patterns where others see only meaningless data.' It was as if he had set off a light bulb in my head. Suddenly, I had a frame through which to look at the future. At that moment, I knew I wanted to be like him—someone who could see patterns where others saw only chaos, someone who could inspire others to think differently.

Thanks to John Naisbitt, I found my frame for the future. It was about globalizing Indian thought. It was a simple yet profound framework that guided my academic and popular writing for years. I felt grateful to Naisbitt for those moments of inspiration and insight.

Looking back, I realize that Naisbitt was more than just a man who predicted the future. He was a man who shaped the future. I was left with a lingering question: can I do that too?

When rejection became my inspiration

Professor Sitangshu Chakraborty was my mentor and guide at IIM Calcutta. He introduced me to the world of Indian thought through the work and wisdom of four of India's greatest icons: Mahatma Gandhi, Rabindranath Tagore, Aurobindo Ghosh and Swami Vivekananda.

Prof. Chakraborty and I, with two other accomplished colleagues, co-created the Management Centre for Human Values, probably the first entrepreneurial attempt inside an IIM to put together a corporate-funded self-sustaining centre.

Professor Chakraborty was a stickler for propriety and top-down management. He seemed to like me but was often upset with my idiosyncratic ways and occasional rebellion. When I returned from Harvard, flushed with the glory of my first internationally published book, *Leading Consciously*, something strange happened.

I remember the moment as if it were yesterday. The air was thick with tension as my mentor, Professor Sitangshu Chakraborty (or SKC, as we all called him), gave me some unexpected advice: 'You have become too big for a small centre at IIM.' At first, I was confused. Had I done something wrong? Was he trying to compliment me? But, as I thought about it more, I realized that this was a not-so-subtle way of saying that he was about to fire me from my job at IIM Calcutta. Perhaps, he was letting me go so that I did not have to hide in his shadow.

It was a tough pill to swallow. SKC had been my guide and mentor, and I had looked up to him for years. But I knew that I couldn't let this rejection get me down. Instead, I used it as inspiration.

I resigned from my job at IIM Calcutta and set out to continue the work of institutionalizing Indian thought, something that SKC had pioneered in his own way. It wasn't easy—I faced plenty of rejection and scepticism along the way—but I knew that this was what I was meant to do.

Looking back, I'm grateful for that moment of rejection. It pushed me out of my comfort zone and gave me the drive to keep going even when things got tough. And I know that SKC would be proud of me for carrying on his legacy in my own way. In the realm of leadership, rejection often becomes a profound source of inspiration. It sets you on a path of introspection and expands the horizons of your learning. Through rejection, you discern what doesn't align with your path, and it equips you to approach life from fresh perspectives, paving the way for positive change.

2

Arc of Aspiration

As a child, my curiosity coexisted with introversion. I barely spoke in class. My time was mostly spent sensing and observing the world. One was gifted with vivid memory to reconstruct experiences. Gradually, a keen sense of humour developed in me by observing the adult world's foolishness and foibles.

I wondered how my aunts and uncles hushed up when interesting topics like scandals, illness, death, marriages, or family disputes were brought up. It became evident that adults frequently underestimate the perceptive abilities of children, and this realization intrigued me even more.

I started writing in fourth standard. My first essay, published in a newspaper run by my father, was largely adapted from a British writer's essay. When my father painted the town red by talking about the literary genius in me, I did not have the heart to tell him the whole truth. That would have shattered his dreams. However,

I vowed to be a writer in my own right so that I could prove my father right. And truly I did. In the long run, I ended up writing several books and articles that were published internationally.

From a very young age, the simple things of life have awed me. Friends from my school days would often observe every move I made. I became a bit of an icon in their eyes. Sutanu Mitra often recalls my visits to his home: 'Debashis would visit my home when our college classes were over, sometimes by himself, and park his all-weather bicycle (weather-beaten) against a bushy red rangoon plant in the southern part of the garden; and then, taking his dusty leather sandals off, he would stroll around the neatly mowed lawns. With unedited joy and a radiant smile on his lips, he would take in the squeezy softness of the grass under each light tread. "Wonderful!" he would say, standing in the middle of the garden, placing his hands in his over-creased jeans pockets and moving his toe in an arc over the grass in front.'

My childhood friend and classmate, Pompa Moitra, recalls, 'We were a close-knit batch of twelve students. The stunted strength of the class enhanced the development of a strong bond of friendship and fellow feeling among us. As we progressed through each class, this attachment grew stronger. Debashis had been an inseparable part of this bond of cooperation and companionship. Though quiet and reflective, he extended his helping hand and encouraged the ones who lagged a little behind to boost their morale. Maybe it was the initiation of the making of what he is today, a teacher of global acclaim and influence, a pathbreaker.'

Another classmate, Saibal Ghosh, recalls an incident relating to a surprise test we were going to be given in our vernacular language class. After a few minutes of the class pleading with the teacher to defer the test, she appeared to be relenting when Ghosh, who was very alarmed at having to take a surprise test, said, in a surprisingly loud voice, 'No test today'. At once the offended teacher got up from her seat and said sternly, 'I am going to give the test here and now.' Ghosh was the recipient of many a dirty glares from the rest of the class, and one student sitting close to him even whispered to him what dire consequences were going to come his way. Apparently, it was only I, after glancing his way, who did not say anything to him. I seemed to be the only one who stood by him against a hostile class. 'It is not an idle coincidence that you are what you are today,' Saibal tells me.

After schooling, I was working on my MBBS degree at a local medical school, much to my father's pride. After a few months, I informed my father that the medical degree was not for me and that I could not continue it. Unsurprisingly, my father was extremely disappointed and upset at my decision, and I ended up being confined to my room for a whole day as he tried his best to persuade me out of my decision. Finally, he relented.

College days, however, were filled with uncertainty and self-doubt. I explored different fields, including commerce and chemistry and finally settled on English literature at the best liberal arts college in my hometown. This journey allowed me to experience interdisciplinary learning. Enrolling in a BA degree programme in English literature, I not only graduated with honours but also secured the top position in the university, setting a record for the highest marks in English that stood for many years.

Subsequently, I pursued an MA in English literature at Jawaharlal Nehru University in New Delhi. During my time there, I thrived in my eclectic choice of subjects, gaining a national context and an international perspective. At JNU, I became a member of Free Thinkers, providing an alternative to the dominant left politics on campus. Additionally, I developed a substantial fan base and wrote popular columns for newspapers and magazines.

I passed out of the university and cleared a number of competitive examinations for employment and finally chose to join the General Insurance Corporation of India, where I was assigned to New India Assurance. Due to the impending retirement of my father and the need to provide for my family, I had to make the difficult decision of forgoing my dream of attending Oxford with an Inlaks scholarship. Taking up a job became a necessity during that time. Rashmi Iyer, principal officer and director at Global Insurance Brokers Pvt. Ltd., says, 'The postings were like being thrown in the sea—some got lucky with softer assignments but most of us were handy scapegoats for the most thankless assignments. The young blood in us did not mind any of this as we were highly charged. Destiny has plans for us that are unknown to us, and it brings out the best. This cannot be truer than with Debashis. His stint at National Insurance Academy marked a turning point in his career and from where he has never looked back. I'm so proud to see him become a prolific thought leader.'

Now, let me tell you a little bit about my three obsessions: sports, cinema and food. I used to play quite a bit of cricket and football during my school and college days. As an opening batsman, I became known for carrying my bat through the innings, employing a straight bat to defend and score runs. Sunil

Gavaskar, the maestro of the game, greatly inspired me with his elegant straight drives and unwavering focus. Years later, I had the incredible opportunity to meet Gavaskar in person and expressed that he was like my Arjuna. To my delight, he agreed to write a review for my best-selling book, *Invincible Arjuna*. In 2012, the name Arjun became highly popular for boys in India, and I had speculated that if every father with a child named Arjun bought my book, it would be great for business. Well, it is another matter altogether that my hunch was proved right.

For a Bengali growing up in a suburban town, football was more like a recreational staple in my diet. The school football field held me to ransom, and I played as a centre-forward for my school and for the local (para) teams, scoring several crucial match-winning goals. Sports, for me, was more than a pastime. It was about discovering the creative aspect of my physical and mental capacities. It was also about bonding with both friends and enemies. The football field was a great equalizer to sort out sibling rivalry! My brother, not so good in studies, was the athletic type. His skill on the football field far exceeded that of mine.

Good films, too, drew me like a moth to a flame. I did a film appreciation course at the Film and Television Institute of India, Pune, moonlighting from my first corporate job. We had eminent directors like Basu Chatterjee, Mani Kaul and Govind Nihalini as our teachers. They treated us to a feast of films, and I became acquainted with the soul of Indian cinema. I am still a film buff and watch at least one movie a week.

My other abiding passion, given my Bengali roots, is, of course, food! K.C. Badhok, who used to work for the Indian

Revenue Service, says, 'I've known Debashis for thirty-five years, since 1987, when we were training together in Bombay. Once we were having lunch at a restaurant in South Bombay; it was then that we came to know of his fondness for fish and his vast and oceanic knowledge about fish.' Just as the Chinese skilfully wield chopsticks, Bengalis have an innate dexterity of fingers with which we sort out the fine bones of a fish, a culinary bond that resonates deep within our culture.

I am a strong advocate of building bridges with people and firmly believe that ego and self-centricity are the walls that alienate people from each other. My relationships with my colleagues, family, friends and myself are an outcome of this belief. My friends have often given me some of the best advice I have ever gotten, both personally and professionally. One of them said that I wrote much better than I spoke. That was so true. My awareness of this made me focus more on writing—as a result of which I have several books under my belt—rather than too many speaking engagements which I judiciously avoid. I derive great joy from spotting both similarities and dissimilarities in the things I observe, drawing life lessons from even the smallest happenings around me. Sheer observation, according to me, allows deep thought to find expression through us.

One principle I learnt is that 'best' can be the enemy of 'good'. Striving to be the absolute best can sometimes hinder us from achieving true fulfilment. Instead, I advocate focusing on being the best version of ourselves without comparing ourselves to others. When we let go of the obsession with being the best, among many out there, we can find contentment and satisfaction in our endeavours.

Think of two real achievers: the Buddha and Beethoven. One was seeking enlightenment and the other was trying to achieve sublimity through music. Whom were they competing against? None. They were only trying to be as good as they could be. Ironically, both reached their peaks when the peaks no longer mattered to them. The Buddha found enlightenment when he was on the very edge of death. Beethoven composed his best music when he was deaf—he could not even hear the thunderous applause of his audiences that his symphonies evoked. Trying to be as good as you can be does not mean lowering your benchmarks or goals. All you have to do is to stop obsessing over being the best. A stroke of luck can make one the best among many contenders. The others can be as good as they can be and still find fulfilment in their activities.

Emphasizing the connection between management and music, I have named all the students' hostels at IIM Kozhikode after the ragas of Indian classical music: *Arabhi*, *Jog*, *Kamboj*, *Kalyani* and *Hamsadhawni*.

India's world-renowned violinist, L. Subramaniam says, 'I have visited numerous music colleges, yet I have not witnessed a single building named after ragas in any of them.' I deeply appreciate his comment. Piped instrumental music is played intermittently in the campus corridors. Maanvi Ahuja, an alumnus of IIMK, fondly remembers, 'Debashis was the only teacher who used music as a tool to invoke deeper thought. I remember how he was ahead of his time in bringing music to the classroom in those days.'

There is surely a connection between management and music. Management is much more than the crunching of numbers based on rational principles. Management involves navigating the world of emotions, harmonizing the minds of people, and understanding the rhythms of the workplace and the cycles of business. Management is closer to art than it is to science. Corporate life is more of a multi-dimensional dance than the unidimensional movement of assembly lines. Appreciation and understanding of music develop our sensitivity and helps us tune into the subtle aspects of corporate life. When asked by a student about the relevance of my use of music in management classes, my dean, G. Sridhar, responded, 'You have to face the music if you don't perform in management.' How true!

I accept that academic life is now reduced to the creation of mental real estate. Just as the real estate business is all about location, location and location, academic careers are now about publication, publication and publication. Real academic life has to do with creating the right architecture for learning. We are here to unleash the flow of curiosity by propagating the culture of questioning rather than creating embankments of knowledge.

The subject of happiness has stirred the imagination of corporations around the world. Happiness, for me, is the flow of life between thoughts. We get heart blocks as a result of the hardening of our arteries. Similarly, we develop mind blocks from the hardening of categories! Happiness and unhappiness are mind-made categories. No other entity in nature—a plant, a panda or a python—seeks happiness. The rest of nature simply follows the urge for self-preservation by being what they are. A plant does not live in the future, and a python does not desire to belong to another reptile category.

Happiness has become a trillion-dollar enterprise with a whole paraphernalia of products, services, authors and coaches.

The pursuit of happiness is the surest way to find unhappiness, like a dog chasing its tail. Happiness is what remains when you loosen up the hard categories in your mind: yesterday versus today; effort versus results; likes versus dislikes. What remains then is the dynamic flow of life, with its crests and troughs. Happiness is about going with the flow.

Happiness has a deep bond with mind management. While you struggle to get out of bed in the morning to do your workout, you are losing the battle with your mind. The only thing you can control in this vast universe is your mind. Even your body is beyond your control as it is hurtled through space by a spinning earth. The world outside your mind—your circumstances, your situations, your people—functions independently of you. You have no control over it either. But the mind is a multipurpose vehicle that you can learn to ride and control.

The mind has four dimensions: rationality, emotional response, willpower and ingenuity. They are like four numbers on a combination lock. You have to arrange those four elements in the right order to unlock your potential. All you can do is regulate the mind so it falls in line with your intention. The desires of the mind accelerate your will. The rational mind acts as a brake. Emotions fuel your outward actions. Ingenuity guides your actions through unexplored paths. Learn to manage your mind's magical powers. Surrender what you cannot control to the larger, universal mind.

Happiness is an event. Todd Rose, director of the Mind, Brain and Education Program at Harvard, traces the root of the word happiness to 'hap', as in 'happening', in 'mishap' (a troublesome occurrence) or in 'haphazard' (misaligned).

Sitting over a steaming cup of tea one Sunday morning, I began to think of happiness as an occurrence that happens inside us when our moods, modes and mindscapes align with something deep inside our psyche that is larger than our known selves. I discover happiness looking at the Wayanad hills in north Kerala. It is not as if those rocks on the hills bring me happiness. Rather, happiness is that expansive and undiscovered happening within me that shows up in the company of the crisp mountain air. It is not easy to find happiness within oneself. But it is truly impossible to find it anywhere else.

As part of his first entrepreneurial venture, Mukund Trivedy, national head of communication and media relations at Hindustan Coca-Cola Beverages (HCCB), once organized a conclave on the subject of 'happy workplace'. He wanted me to be a speaker at the event, and I readily agreed, even though he did not have any sponsors at the time, nor even a team or money to pull off such a big event. During my speech when someone asked me why happiness needed to be promoted in the workplace at all, I said that just as atoms have protons and electrons, organizations also have morons. And if you ask these morons what makes them happy, they will tell you that making others unhappy makes them happy. Trivedy remembers how there was a big turnout and credits me with stealing the show with my 'disarming sense of wit and humour'.

In the realm of enterprise, where hard work intertwines with health, a symphony of well-being and happiness emerges. Unfortunately, we rush to take up high-paid jobs at the cost of our physical and mental health. Our work lives, akin to the crushing machines that process sugarcanes, present a paradox. At one end, a vibrant, juicy soul enters—brimming with energy and youthfulness—only to emerge from the other side as a worn-out pulp, drained by the grind of routine and the whirlwind of week-long endeavours.

Within this cycle, the hapless worker finds solace in moments of laughter, slapping his thighs with mirth as he envisions his boss ensnared in a hospital bed. 'I'd be happy if my boss lands in the emergency room with broken bones,' he roars, a devilish delight in his eyes. Strangely, someone's unhappiness becomes the source of his joy, a peculiar alchemy of emotions. For others, the shrine of happiness resides within their stomachs, nourished by the anticipation of lunch breaks, where motivation thrives in culinary delights. Such is the tapestry of human emotions woven within the intricate fabric of work-life, where happiness dances with the shadows of discontent, and the heart's melodies resonate with the rhythms of daily toil.

3

The Class Act

Author George Bernard Shaw, in his 1903 play *Man and Superman*, said that 'he who can, does; he who cannot, teaches'. Generally speaking, it sounds gloomy for educators, with many feeling rather blue in the social and economic pecking orders. These educators include many school principals, who feel cynical about their calling.

Once, during a leadership workshop for school principals, I heard a rib-tickling anecdote. A geography teacher was confidently telling his students that the mighty river Ganga originated in the Himalayas and eventually merged with the Arabian Sea. Little did he know that the school principal, ever vigilant during his rounds, was eavesdropping.

The principal couldn't resist correcting the teacher, 'Hey, hey! The Ganga actually terminates in the Bay of Bengal, not the Arabian Sea!'

Caught off guard, the flustered teacher retorted, 'Yes, yes, I know that! But if you raised my salary by 25 per cent, I swear river Ganga would miraculously change its course!'

We sometimes encounter classroom characters that would give stand-up comedians a run for their money. The noble profession of a teacher has often turned out to be the last resort of ignoble characters. Nevertheless, let us not forget that teachers have been esteemed leaders of human societies for centuries, revered for their vital role in shaping minds.

The Buddha, renowned as a teacher among other things, dedicated himself to illuminating humanity, with profound insights, into its true essence. Mahatma Gandhi, advocating the principle of *nai talim* (basic education), emphasized the inseparable connection between knowledge and labour, valuing both intellectual and manual work alike. India's first president, Sarvapalli Radhakrishnan, a remarkable scholar, is honoured on September 5 (Teacher's Day). On this day, not only do we celebrate his birth, but I also fondly recall another lesser-known person—myself—as we share the same birthday. Coincidentally, my wife Aditi was born on September 3, leading our family to celebrate our birthdays together on September 4—a convenient midpoint for busy family members. Reflecting on this special occasion, Abdul Kalam, the eleventh president of India, expressed in an exclusive interview with *The Hindu* newspaper on Teachers' Day in 2013, 'If people remember me as a good teacher, that will be the greatest honour for me.' The role of teaching has transformed humanity into a potent driving force behind civilization's advancement.

The art and craft of teaching

Indeed, great teaching is far more than a mere technique; it is an art and a craft that involves coaxing curiosity, nurturing the learner's spirit, and embarking on a delightful journey of discovery.

Picture this: my grandmother, a lady who never set foot in a school, became one of my first teachers. Through her extraordinary stories, she ignited the fire of my imagination. Among the many stories she shared with me, the tale of Yaksha and Yudhisthira from The Mahabharata remains etched in my memory as if painted by a master's hand. Let me recall that story for you:

The demigod Yaksha, known for his questioning prowess, engaged the truth-loving Yudhisthira in a riveting question-and-answer session. Yaksha asked:

'What is the strangest thing that you find in human nature?'
Yudhisthira reflected and replied:
'The strangest thing that I find in human beings is that everyone knows that they will die one day. But, they go about their business as though they will never die.'

Yudhisthira spoke about the paradox of countless individuals marching towards death while harbouring an unwavering belief in their immortality. A curious contemplation indeed, hinting at an unblinking light of consciousness beyond the ephemeral human body.

The rishis—they could be deemed as one of the great teachers of India—have often called this undying consciousness inside us our real nature. They described human beings as '*amritasya putra*' or, the offspring of immortality. In this quest to unravel the very essence of human existence, we turn our gaze towards the fast-vanishing breed of gurus, the unsung heroes who toil tirelessly behind the scenes, shaping lives and moulding minds.

In India, great teachers evolved as *acharyas*. The Sanskrit word *'achar'* means practice. Acharya is 'the one who practices', and her preaching follows whatever she practices. So, to gain credibility as a teacher, it makes sense that a guru or acharya is expected to have direct experience of the results of the knowledge that she is imparting to students. In the modern sense, if somebody teaches automobile engineering without having ever driven or seen a car, he/she is unlikely to be a great acharya.

I had the immense privilege of encountering such a guru, my chemistry teacher, Aparesh Bhattacharya. He was the vice principal of Scottish Church College, Kolkata, and a man of exceptional insight. Beyond the confines of his subject matter, he lived the very teachings he imparted, leaving an indelible impression upon all who had the fortune to witness his captivating chemistry classes. With the dexterity of a master painter's brushstrokes, he breathed life into complex reactions, recognizing the immense power of words, which can shape the destinies of generations. He would transform a typical laboratory session into a colourful and riotous ecstasy.

'Tell me the colour of burning calcium?'

'What? Brick red. Oh, that's textbook stuff.'

'What else?'

'Shade of lipstick?'

'Fresh blood oozing out of a wound?'

Aparesh Bhattacharya urged us to transcend the chains of rote learning and soar wholeheartedly into the wonders of the world. Who would have thought that burning calcium could be compared to the shade of lipstick or fresh blood from a wound?

Teachers who place themselves on a pedestal may carry a pumpkin-sized ego. I've heard that in Japan, calling oneself a teacher is seen as an act of arrogance. A true teacher, however, always remains a learner at heart. They must view their teachings from the diverse perspectives of their students rather than adhering to a rigid and narrow framework. Embracing this open-mindedness and being willing to adapt makes humility an integral part of a great teacher's way of life.

Here is what one of my maverick students from IIM Lucknow, Gaurav Mittal, said about his first impressions of taking a course I taught: 'Deb Chat's sessions on self-awareness and self-inquiry shifted the focus from doing to being. Once, he asked us to observe the space between thoughts, which was my first experience of being in observation of the mind. Needless to say, he was received with a fair amount of scepticism in the beginning, as the majority of us came from a hard, outwardly skill-focused background in engineering. I am sure that over the years, a lot of that preliminary scepticism has turned into appreciation as we have encountered life in its many forms. He offered us an amazing non-judgemental space of self-expression and development.'

Literacy, numeracy or ecstasy?

During my school days, classrooms were like courtrooms. You could feel like a prisoner on trial, being questioned by everyone. For instance, the algebra teacher, whose face bore a barren look akin to the Sahara Desert, would ask:

'Tell me what is a quadratic equation?'

One need not know how a quadratic equation came into existence. All one did was mumble some vaguely remembered alphabets and numbers that were memorized and lodged in the cerebral cortex. Learning was mere cerebration rather than celebration.

Yet, for me, the fulfilment of a learning experience lay not in acquiring numeracy or literacy, but in experiencing ecstasy. The classical Indian expression for such an experience is 'ananda'. Ananda is that eureka moment we experience when the doors of our perception are flung open. Great teachers have a magical ability to awaken dormant facets of our minds through unexpected questions that beckon us into the depths of contemplation. One such question from my school days that still lingers in my mind:

'If livelihood is for life, then do you wonder, what is life for?'

In one of my classes, a teacher shared a profound insight that left a lasting impact. He said that if all the oceans were to disappear, the vast landmass would be united seamlessly, transcending all divisive national borders. This, he explained, exemplified the power of a holistic perspective that could weave together seemingly contradictory concepts, much like the beautiful harmony of art and technology observed in the majestic bamboo tree. The bamboo tree, he continued, serves as both a biological pump, drawing water much like a mechanical pump, and a work of art, gracefully swaying through storms, displaying resilience, and captivating the eye with its beauty. The convergence of these dual aspects—the scientific and the aesthetic—in the bamboo tree demonstrates the remarkable potential when different elements come together in perfect balance and unity. There is truth inherent in beauty. My daughter Shrishti, who designs communication for entities around the world, often says, 'I cannot un-see the lack of harmony in some of these smartphone photographs.' Her eyes are trained to see and nurture beauty in ordinary objects. True to her name, Shrishti turned out to be a creative artist.

In a world, there are as many perspectives as the number of teachers, who together, can offer a panorama of views instead of just one side of a topic. The moments spent with my guru were nothing short of sheer delight, for he understood the profound significance of ecstasy at the very heart of the learning process. Those eureka moments of revelation liberate the mind and stir the pursuit of buried joy within us.

The rise of the soft power of education

In the changing landscape of education, the new face of leadership is softer and less formal. This shift is exemplified by three remarkable women I met during one of my visits to the US with the education minister of India. These three women were then leading major US universities: Drew Faust, the first female president of Harvard University; Susan Hockfield, the first woman and life scientist to lead MIT; and Renu Khator, the first Indian American woman to become the chancellor and president of the University of Houston.

These leaders exemplify the strength of informality and the embrace of the gentle-yet-influential force of education. Drew Faust, a passionate advocate of humanistic inquiry, emphasized the importance of introspection and self-awareness, guiding us on a transformative journey from uncertainty to wisdom. In the face of global economic challenges, she cherished our shared human heritage. Similarly, Susan Hockfield of MIT embodied a new vision for higher education, advocating for the seamless integration of knowledge across various disciplines. This approach gave birth to innovative fields such as biomechanics, nuclear medicine and conscious capitalism. The fluidity and exchange of knowledge, often referred to as 'flowledge', defied the traditional confines that had historically limited academic growth.

The rise of the creative, whole-brain valuing soft cortical skills and big-picture perception, challenged the dominance of analytical left-brain structures. In this transformation, women like Renu Khator shone as leaders, bringing diverse perspectives in recruiting faculty. Renu Khator told me that she was her husband's boss's boss. Here, the recruitment strategy for professors for her university included inviting a whole department full of a bright professor's team to join her university together. Renu's journey from a small town in Uttar Pradesh to the highest echelons of American education highlighted the triumph of the soft power of India within the once-insular corner office of American academia.

Classroom without walls

The true classroom lies in the minds of the students, where thoughts, perceptions, and emotions converge, and create the essence of the learning experience. Great educators empower students to think for themselves by providing the space to learn through their own experiences.

Professor Yash Pal was one of India's most iconic teachers. With a doctorate in physics from the MIT, he was an institution builder and a great teacher. He could simplify complex subjects with utmost ease. He demonstrated a simple truth—a good teacher explains, but a great teacher enlivens science subjects. If a student asked an average physics teacher what gravity was; he would get an explanation that would be abstract and mathematical. Here is how Professor Yash Pal would explain the concept of gravity to his students animatedly.

He would draw a circle representing the circumference of the earth. Then he would draw pictures of tiny human figures standing around the circle. He would point to a human form on the top of the circle and ask, 'The little human is standing upright right at the top. That is not so surprising. But look at the fellow standing upright at the bottom of the earth. Do you now know what gravity is all about?'

Professor Yash Pal would thus immerse the whole class in the mystery of the gravitational force.

Great teachers, such as Professor Yash Pal, highlight the difference between the explicable and the inexplicable, combining logic and magic, igniting moments of revelation that take the student to the core of knowledge.

Several years later, during my second five-year term as the director of IIM Kozhikode, I had the privilege of commissioning a classroom that I called 'gurukul for gurus'. This was a sunlit classroom, panelled by glass walls on four sides and arched with a very high brick ceiling. We put grass under the feet, vertical gardens on the sides and live trees inside the classroom. The teachers and students would sit down on low wooden seats in a circular arrangement. This natural ambience of the classroom soon became a favourite at IIM Kozhikode. Students hurried to remove their shoes to flock to this forty-seater class. Our gurukul awakened the contemplative capacity of our students in the lap of nature.

Education, a passionate pursuit and a pilgrimage to our consciousness, holds the key to unlocking the wellsprings of creativity. By shedding the masks of ego and embracing authenticity, we tap into the core of our creative source. Creative ideas, born from the randomness and unpredictability of the universe, can lead to innovations that shape the future. Embracing creativity means embracing the art of de-materialization, turning something into nothingness to bring forth new possibilities.

As we embrace the changing face of education, we must dismantle the barriers between disciplines and nurture the creative flow of knowledge. This 'flowledge' challenges the separation between science, arts and aesthetics, promoting a more holistic approach to learning. India's National Education Policy acknowledges and emphasizes the rebirth of this fluidity of knowledge systems in education. The great rishis of the Upanishads had long foreseen knowledge as a 'flow process' when they exclaimed, '*Neti, Neti, Chrareibeti* [Not this, not this, move on]!'

4

Facing Facts

There are several ways in which educational institutions are different from the more common organizational structures in business, industry and trade. Teaching and learning are the primary responsibilities and goals of educational institutions. More than just passing along knowledge or information, teaching involves diverse activities. For teaching to promote personality development, it requires the formation of a close relationship between the teacher and the student, with an emphasis on independence, the ability to make independent decisions and a sense of personal responsibility. It is not surprising that there is this negative notion in society that any failure, flaw or decline in any part of national life is attributable to teachers.

There are many unknowns in the process of learning. The desire to learn, the learning process and the consequences of learning are all somewhat unpredictable. For instance, learning can sometimes have unexpected effects on a person's viewpoint and attitude. Exam results are routinely evaluated, and failing an exam could have negative consequences for the student. The majority of these adjustments entail teachers being given new responsibilities in areas where they lack the requisite training. Environmental changes—in particular, technological and social developments; increased responsibility; and, finally yet importantly, the gradual loss of the professional authority of the teacher—have a considerable impact on the management of the educational institution.

My colleagues often remark that the merry upward journey for IIMK started during my first term as the director of the institute. Since then, they said, the sky has been the limit (for the institute). They note that several pioneering achievements have been lined up for IIMK since then and that the institute saw its golden era from 2009 to 2014.

IIMK wears the hat of being the first IIM to increase female student intake to 54 per cent for its flagship post-graduate MBA programme. My conviction to bring diversity to the forefront at IIMs bore fruit when other IIMs followed suit. IIMK became the first business school to offer a two-year online executive post-graduate programme and the first IIM to be accredited for the executive post-graduate programme by the London-based Association of MBAs (AMBA). This international accreditation certification puts the institute on par with the very best in the global management education hub. During my first stint as director, the institute entered into an MoU with Yale University, New Haven, USA, along with IIT Kanpur, for the exchange of scientific, academic and technical information; for the conduct of joint workshops, seminars, courses and conferences related to academic leadership; and for the establishment of two Centres of Excellence in Academic Leadership (CEEAL) in India. The institute led twenty-nine vice-chancellors of universities and directors of IITs and IIMs to Yale University for a two-week academic leadership workshop.

In 2012, I created the Museum of Indian Business History, later named the Indian Business Museum (IBM), which added to the glory of the institute. Trade, commerce, business and industry have a varied as well as rich tradition and a vast history in the Indian subcontinent, but no business history museums or archives have been attempted or created in India thus far. This pointed to a dire need for a national business history museum in India. The vision at IIMK was to create a world-class national museum of Indian business history to shape the aspirations of young entrepreneurs and propel forward business entrepreneurship in the country. The mission has been to collect, display and preserve an outstanding collection of artefacts, objects, sculptures, photographs, historical documents, letters, miniature models, videos, audios, digital objects and books, etc., showcasing the wealth of Indian business history for posterity; to portray and display systematically the development of trade, commerce and business in the Indian subcontinent over the past several centuries; and to inspire and ignite entrepreneurial skills and business innovation among the talented youth of India. The objective has also been to acknowledge, befittingly and consciously, the contribution of India's business leaders and corporates in the making of India, to inculcate the spirit of innovation and business entrepreneurship among the youth of India, and to inspire aspiring and budding business entrepreneurs in India.

IIMK was the first business school to reduce the annual fee for the post-graduate programme, providing significant relief to economically disadvantaged students. Being historically known as the frontrunner in bringing about a nationwide change in thinking across institutes of national importance to encourage gender diversity and inclusive growth, IIMK has left no stone unturned in this respect. Its rollback of tuition fees by Rs 30,000 in 2012 was a radical step in the direction of making higher education accessible to all deserving students based on merit, thus combining equity and excellence.

On 16 January 2011, IIMK conducted a workshop on 'Sustaining Leadership and Governance' on the campus for the Government of Kerala. As the director of IIMK, I presided over the workshop, engaging Mr Oommen Chandy, the then chief minister of Kerala, members of the legislative assembly, and cabinet ministers. I spoke at length on the concept of 'timeless leadership', which is ever-evolving. The goal of timeless leadership is to teach people management concepts and techniques that can be used to draw up and carry out strategies in different functional areas. Mr Chandy commented at the end of the day-long workshop, 'Never was a day better spent than this one. There will never be another one quite like you.'

I recall an interesting incident that happened during the workshop. I asked Mr Chandy, 'Why don't you conduct your cabinet meetings standing up? That way your cabinet members will have 20 per cent more blood circulation in their brains as compared to meetings conducted sitting on a chair. Besides, the decision-making process is likely to be faster.'

'That is exactly what I do—holding outbound meetings standing up!' Mr Chandy said gleefully.

'That is why they call you an outstanding Chief Minister!' I retorted.

Mr Chandy and his entire cabinet colleagues had a hearty laugh upon hearing my rejoinder! A gracious man! A large-hearted CM! My colleagues at IIMK and I mourned his passing away this year. RIP Oomen Chandy!

I am the founder-editor of *IIM Kozhikode Society & Management Review*, a biannual journal that aims to connect the management community—academics, businesses, public institutions, non-governmental organizations and the government—by motivating research and publishing rigorous, clear and widely accessible articles on business management and the broader society. This journal is a member of the Committee on Publication Ethics (COPE). This is the only journal from any Indian management school indexed in both the Chartered Association of Business Schools (ABS 2021 (ABS 2)) and the Australian Business Deans Council (ABDC 2019 (C)) lists.

The golden era of the institute, which supposedly began in 2009, attained its ultimate sheen during 2018–2022. Established in June 2016, IIMK's business incubator, LIVE, completed five years. It has now emerged as a collaborative platform helping transform innovative ideas into business ventures that aim to have significant economic and social impact. Having incubated eighty-nine start-ups with a high success rate of 40 per cent, LIVE Incubates has raised Rs 37 crore to date and generated revenue of Rs 50 crore in a short period. Set up with the support of the Department of Science and Technology, the government of India, the centre is envisioned to function as a business incubator to create a national centre of excellence that promotes innovation, new business ventures and entrepreneurship. As an on-campus incubator, it stands to gain immensely from the work and advice of faculty members and students, the institute's research and knowledge base, its alumni, institutional networks and other resources.

IIM Kozhikode conducted two special training programmes in leadership and management for senior diplomats and government officials from over twenty countries in collaboration with the Ministry of External Affairs (GoI) under the Indian Technical and Economic Cooperation (ITEC) programme, on the themes 'Leadership 4.0: Management & Governance in the Emerging World of Disruption' and 'Doing Business in India: An India Immersion Programme' (2019). India's biggest contribution to the world has been knowledge, and the country has a lot to offer when it comes to innovations and community-driven initiatives. These ITEC programmes, with their intensive take on leadership and management, will equip the participants with unparalleled skills.

IIM Kozhikode and Mangalore Refineries and Petrochemicals Ltd announced a special drive to support women entrepreneurs in the country. This initiative, labelled 'La Eve' (meaning 'The Woman') aims to identify innovative, promising women-founded start-ups and provide them with comprehensive start-up support programmes. Selected women-led start-ups have received seed funding of up to Rs 25 lakh. IIMK LIVE would identify and incubate female-led start-ups, giving them access to the institute's intellectual, network and infrastructural resources. MRPL would provide seed funding assistance from the start-up funding initiative under the Start-up India Program. IIM Kozhikode has always recognized the potential of women in management practice and business leadership. Having been at the forefront of starting several initiatives that provide fair opportunities to women in pursuing careers in management, La Eve is yet another initiative in the country to harness the potential of women and help them actively contribute to the country's economy.

The fourth (2019) and fifth (2022) editions of IIMK's Book Donation Drive handed out a total of 37,000 books worth Rs 1.85 crore to sixty colleges in the Malabar region of Kerala as part of the institute's CSR drive. This programme is part of the institute's efforts to create 'social capital' by being relevant and sensitive to the communities to whom it is accountable. Social reputation is a product of the intellectual and social capital that organizations hold. I hope this small initiative will enthuse and inspire young minds with the priceless knowledge embedded in the thousands of books being received by them and ignite a spark in them. The fruits of this will come back as new and renewed energy to strengthen our society.

Business incubators at IIM Kozhikode and the National Institute of Design, Ahmedabad, collaborated to offer design thinking and design experience for start-ups. This is the first time in India that a business incubator hosted at a business school has struck an alliance with another one at a design school (2020). The MoU brings two institutes of national importance in two diverse domains—design and management—together to collaborate and create offerings that may boost the innovation and venture-support ecosystem in the country. This could make it easier for different groups to connect and build a stronger start-up ecosystem in India. As I write this, Appasaheb Naikal, librarian at IIMK, is trying to create IIMK book kiosks at bus stands and other waiting places in the city to promote a reading culture among the people and encourage them to cultivate reading as a habit.

IIMK hosted the first international conclave on 'Globalizing Indian Thought' in 2020. GIT 2020 was inaugurated by the prime minister of India, Narendra Modi; also present at the occasion were Vinay Sahasrabuddhe, president of the Indian Council for Cultural Relations (ICCR); Kiran Bedi, former lieutenant governor of Puducherry; Sri Sri Ravi Shankar, spiritual leader; Arun Maira, former member of the Planning Commission of India; Prabhu Chawla, journalist; and many more leading lights from diverse fields. IIM Kozhikode embraced 'globalizing *Indian thought*' as its institutional mission a decade ago. Over the years, the institute has fostered and nurtured various elements of the Indian ethos in management and leadership. In India, globalization has, for a long time, been synonymous with Westernization. Indian thought does have a lot to contribute to conversations on globalization. The churning of ideas with the amalgamation of wisdom and creativity will be an opportunity for inquisitive thinkers to look at Indian thought with a fresh perspective and a renewed mind. From my perspective, Indian leaders thrive on being known as realized beings by embracing the spirit of sustainability and reverence for life.

A five-star GRIHA-rated (Green Rating for Integrated Habitat Assessment) Phase-V 'green campus' was inaugurated at IIM Kozhikode in 2020. It was an initiative of the Ministry of New and Renewable Energy, Government of India, and The Energy and Resources Institute (TERI). Water, soil and energy conservation measures have been extensively adopted in Phase V of the IIMK campus. Solar energy to the tune of 50 kWp (kilowatt peak) is also being harnessed on the campus. Additionally, a rainwater harvesting pond has been developed on the premises to cater to the water requirements of the entire campus. Besides this, the campus also boasts rainwater storage tanks with a storage capacity of forty lakh litres. The harvesting facility also meets any emergency requirements. A sewage treatment plant has also been established on campus to treat effluents, which can then be used for toilet flushing and gardening.

Another highlight of IIMK is the introduction of a state-of-the-art intelligent classroom set-up, which is virtually mic-less, aided by the first-of-its-kind use of ceiling microphones, offering adaptive and intelligent responses to user and room behaviour.

An international team led by an IIM Kozhikode student pioneered a vital digital tool to fight misinformation regarding the COVID-19 pandemic. The website 'COVID FYI' (covidfyi.in) is a one-stop digital directory for all COVID-19-related services and information released by official sources. The website aims to bring the right information from the right sources to the right people, as only official information from government organizations is posted on this platform to ensure authenticity and credibility. The platform is for citizens and government organizations and institutions alike, and provides authenticated information on authorized labs close to the user, designated hospitals, grocery stores, mental health and emergency helplines, task-force team contacts, field officer contacts, emergency doctors to call, fever clinics close to the user, etc. Additional features enable the user to book appointments with doctors, schedule sample collections and find a helpline in an emergency, all the while staying at home and maintaining social distancing, as advised.

The IIM Kozhikode fraternity contributed nearly Rs 1 crore to COVID-19 relief efforts. An amount of Rs 32.09 lakh was donated to the PM Cares fund, of which approximately Rs 7.09 lakh was raised through the voluntary contribution of a day's salary by the director, staff and faculty of the institute. The institute also contributed Rs 25 lakh to the Kerala Chief Minister's Distress Relief Fund (CMDRF) as part of this initiative. Another significant contribution of around Rs 40 lakh was raised by the IIMK Alumni Association.

The National Institutional Ranking Framework (NIRF) introduced by the Ministry of Education in 2015, outlines a methodology to rank institutions across the country and is considered the most authoritative in India. IIM Kozhikode is proud to be consistently ranked as one of the top management institutions in the country. It leapfrogged to come up to the third spot nationally in the National Institutional Ranking Framework (NIRF) 2023 released by the Ministry of Education, thus ABC (IIM Ahmedabad, IIM Bangalore and IIM Calcutta) got changed to ABK (the top three now are IIMs of Ahmedabad, Bangalore and Kozhikode). IIMs are excellent institutions. We build on each other's strengths. The ABC, with their quality of education and the legacy of sixty-plus years, are primed to perform well. To quietly work our way up, replacing IIM Calcutta from the long-standing top three, is a testament to the very ideals IIMs stand for—the pursuit of excellence and to keep going at it. Sometimes the underdogs are hungrier and try harder than the incumbents. Perhaps that's where success stories like IIMK emerge from. The career-best ranking is a testimony to the selfless contribution of its proficient faculty members, efficient administration, magnificent students, alumni and recruiters and ever-supportive governments. The institute will continue to embrace dynamic reforms, encourage research and spread its mission of globalizing Indian thought.

Since its debut in 2020, IIMK's Executive MBA (EMBA) programme has maintained a consistent position among the top 200 universities on the Quacquarelli Symonds (QS) Global EMBA chart, administered by the QS World University Ranking Team. From globalizing Indian thought to finding a place among the world's foremost executive MBA programmes, IIM Kozhikode has reached yet another milestone in higher education. QS consists of a set of indicators grouped under five headings: career progression, academic reputation, employer reputation, executive profile and class diversity. IIMK's flagship PGP program achieved a prestigious position in the top 200 globally and secured a spot in the fourteen-plus category in Asia according to the QS Masters in Management Rankings (PGP) in 2023.

In 2020, IIMK entered into a memorandum of understanding (MoU) with Help Logistics, an organization affiliated with the Kühne Foundation in Schindellegi, Switzerland. The main objective of this collaboration was to revolutionize the efficiency and delivery of humanitarian aid in South Asia. This partnership aimed to address the challenges posed by natural disasters and other man-made disruptions globally. Over one year, the MoU facilitated various activities that focused on optimizing supply chains for the greater benefit of humanity. Amidst the prevailing uncertainty worldwide, the partnership sought to strengthen humanitarian logistics in India and the surrounding region. To achieve this, the collaboration provided consulting services and logistics training to key stakeholders involved in humanitarian crisis response, including United Nations bodies, government institutions, and non-governmental organizations. The joint efforts aimed to create a more streamlined and effective approach to delivering assistance during times of crisis, ensuring that aid reaches those in need promptly and efficiently. By combining the expertise of IIMK and Help Logistics, the partnership made significant strides in enhancing humanitarian efforts and making a positive impact on the lives of people in South Asia.

IIMK repeated history, with more than 60 per cent of students admitted to its flagship PGP programme and its newly launched MBA-LSM programme in 2023 consisting of women.

IIMK began its journey of significantly contributing to the growing trend of female leaders in 2010. There has been a steady rise in its commitment to ensuring gender diversity in the past decade, and its journey towards creating equal opportunities in society and business through the empowerment and advancement of women has been a fulfilling one. The uncertainties and complexities of management in the current business world require a working manager to be able to approach a problem from multiple perspectives. By nurturing the diversity of thought in its classrooms as a result of consciously choosing to create a diverse learning environment, IIMK aims to equip its students with the knowledge and experience that will be essential in sustaining them throughout their professional careers.

In 2023, IIM Kozhikode and Penguin Random House India collaborated to launch an eight-part book series authored by expert IIMK faculty members for new managers, social entrepreneurs and future leaders. The lead book—*Karma Sutras: Leadership and Wisdom in Uncertain Times*—has been authored by me. The ideas in the book stem from the real-life narratives of various thought leaders and my twenty-five years of experience as a scholar and institution builder. Some of the books in the series are:

- *Impactful Communication: Communicate to Conquer* by Deepa Sethi
- *Strategy Huddle: Management Lessons from Sports* by Deepak Dhayanithy
- *Accounting Simplified* by Rachappa Shette
- *Being an Impact Champion: Enacting Corporate Social Consciousness* by Priya Nair Rajeev and Simy Joy
- *Mastering Behaviour: Managing Self and Others* by Payal Anand

Diversity has always been the pivot around which IIMK has successfully reshaped management education in the country over the past decade. Management has also been India's most successful soft power. Our institute's mission of 'Globalizing Indian Thought' closely aligns with the government of India's thrust towards the 'Study in India' programme, which in turn has received a massive boost since the introduction of National Education Policy 2020 and its focus on providing premium education at affordable costs, thereby helping to restore India's role as a *Vishwa Guru*. IIM Kozhikode initiated supernumerary MBA seats for international candidates in 2021 to boost diversity in the institution, and meet the 'Study in India' and NEP 2020 objectives.

IIM Kozhikode bagged a double crown when the EQUIS Accreditation Board voted to confer EQUIS accreditation on IIM Kozhikode on 28 September 2021. It was the fifth IIM and only the sixth management institution in the country to bag the coveted accreditation. EQUIS accreditation is awarded by the European Foundation for Management Development (EFMD), the globally recognized international organization for management development, and has been conferred on prestigious management institutions across the world, like London Business School (United Kingdom) and INSEAD (France). By acquiring EQUIS accreditation, the institute now joins the 'double crown' of accreditation status, enjoyed only by a few institutions in India. We are on the path of acquiring a triple crown with the American Accreditation body, AACSB, coming our way.

To mark an epoch-making twenty-five years of the journey of IIM Kozhikode, the country's premier government business school, India Post (the Department of Posts, Government of India) and IIM Kozhikode jointly released a commemorative 'special cover' in its silver jubilee year of 2021. T. Nirmala Devi, post master general, northern region, India Post, did the honours in the presence of a small representative gathering comprising faculty, staff, students and India Post members, following all social distancing protocols, as the COVID-19 pandemic was still active in the country. Making the occasion all the more special, the IIMK 'Gurukul' was also inaugurated that day and dedicated to the faculty and students of IIM Kozhikode.

In 2021, Vice Admiral Anil Kumar Chawla, PVSM, AVSM, NM, VSM, ADC, flag officer commanding-in-chief, Southern

Naval Command, inaugurated the Navy Pavilion at the IIM Kozhikode Business Museum. The Indian Navy Pavilion is the first facility dedicated to our country's mighty defence forces and has been set up by the Indian Naval Academy at Ezhimala (Kerala). The pavilion is an inspiring space, displaying a replica of the indigenous 'anti-submarine warfare corvette' built by Garden Reach Shipbuilders & Engineers Ltd (GRSE), a government undertaking under the Ministry of Defence. As the museum attracts many young visitors over the academic year, it also lists the various means by which young people can join the force. There are also galleries depicting the Navy's role in providing humanitarian assistance, disaster relief, and the historical sea battles it has won.

IIM Kozhikode established the Centre for Digital Innovation and Transformation (CDiT) in 2021. K. Gopalakrishnan, co founder of Infosys, was the chief guest at the virtual inaugural function. In his inaugural address, Gopalakrishnan, also co-founder of CDiT, congratulated IIM Kozhikode for this initiative and expressed the hope that industry would become an active participant in the centre's activities, being at the intersection of academic and industry activity. He also encouraged the centre to strive for excellence and to come up with sustainable business ideas, creating better products through core research activities to better the lives of people.

IIMK has been recognized as the second most 'innovative' educational institute among institutes of national importance, central universities and Central-Funded Institutes (CFIs) (non-technical) in India. The ARIIA Rankings 2021 were released by Subhas Sarkar, minister of state, Ministry of Education. IIM Kozhikode is the only IIM to feature in the top rankings in this list, which rates institutes on 'Innovation and Entrepreneurship' across seven categories. The Atal Ranking of Institutions on Innovation Achievements (ARIIA) is an initiative of the Ministry of Education, Government of India, to systematically rank all major higher educational institutions and universities in India. A total of 1438 institutions (including IITs, NITs, IISc, IIMs, etc.) participated in the 2021 edition of ARIIA. This was the first edition of ARIIA in which a separate category for non-technical institutions was introduced. In the 2020 edition, IIM Kozhikode was placed in Rank Band A (rank 11–25) under the category of 'Institutes of National Importance, Central Universities, and CFIs'.

IIMK LIVE and Indian Bank inked a landmark MoU to provide loans of up to Rs 50 crore for start-ups under the 'IndSpring Board' scheme in 2022. The loan amount disbursed under the scheme can be used by start-ups to meet their operational and capital expenditures, including working capital, purchase of fixed assets and other expenses. To be chosen for this programme, a start-up would have to be committed to working on innovation, development or improvement of products, processes or services, or have a business model that can be scaled up and has a high chance of creating jobs or wealth.

IIMK and NITI Aayog came together to boost the monitoring and evaluation ecosystem in India by signing a statement of intent (SoI) in 2022. The SoI establishes a framework for cooperative institutional relations to encourage and promote cooperation in the area of technical development. It also aims to support appropriate capacity building and joint studies in the field of monitoring and evaluation of government policies and programmes. In collaboration with the Development Monitoring and Evaluation Office (DMEO), IIM Kozhikode will organize capacity-building programmes, workshops, forums, seminars and other activities to enhance advocacy for monitoring and evaluation of government policies and programmes in the country. This strategic alliance is a manifestation of IIMK's commitment to the three classical values of Indian thought: *Satyam*, *Nityam* and *Purnam*. The conduct of joint research studies on India's development challenges will bring forth the truth of the prevailing status (*Satyam*); further evidence from such studies will assist in informed policy-making, fostering sustainable development (*Nityam*); and all this will eventually make us capable of delivering *Purnam* (wholeness) in our engagement with the research and capacity-building endeavours of DMEO NITI.

IIMK and the Naval Institute of Educational and Training Technology (NIETT), Indian Navy, joined forces in 2022 to collaborate on and exchange best practices in the fields of instructional leadership, educational psychology and management. In the spirit of mutual collaboration, IIMK's Kochi campus will collaborate with the leading training institute of the Indian Navy to seek the cooperation of the best in the industry and the higher education sector to improve the Navy's training practices, help it achieve excellence and enhance the contemporary learning skills of the defence participants. Additionally, this platform offers the faculty of NIETT and selected naval officers the chance to take part in suitable management programmes at IIMK and receive training.

IIMK and the African Asian Rural Development Organization (AARDO) signed an international memorandum of understanding to collaborate and promote sustainable agriculture and rural development in more than thirty member countries by 2022. Thirty-three member countries, including thirty-one in the African Asian Region, are now set to receive renewed research, consultancy, technical and knowledge support from IIMK in promoting sustainable agriculture and rural development practices. Impetus will also be given to advance new knowledge and its sharing, innovative solutions, interventions and capacity enhancement to benefit and strengthen rural communities in the member countries of AARDO.

IIMK and the Institute of Company Secretaries of India (ICSI) signed an MoU for academic collaboration for promoting excellence in common areas of interest and for imparting the knowledge and skills required to operate in the areas of academic programmes, research and training in 2022. The MoU broadly covers activities like specialized training programmes, joint organization of workshops, seminars and continuing education and training programmes, and development of similar academic programmes for practising professionals, corporate executives, faculty members, research scholars and students of both institutes on themes of academic and professional interest. It will also facilitate the exchange of faculty members, journals and course materials, case studies, research publications, and other academic and research projects. Besides this, the MoU also provides for awarding the toppers of programmes at IIM Kozhikode with the ICSI Signature Award Gold Medal and a scholarship to pursue the company secretary course.

In the face of growing competition, technological advancements, and shifting consumer preferences, leaders cannot solely rely on clear vision, incentives and training to ensure business success. Such an assumption poses a risk. Instead, organizations must recognize the need to acquire extensive knowledge to navigate these evolving forces effectively. Thus, every business should aspire to become a learning organization, continuously adapting and growing to thrive in the dynamic landscape.

Learning organizations have been defined by Peter Senge, author of the book *The Fifth Discipline,* which popularized the concept, as places 'where people continually expand their capacity to create the results they truly desire, where new and expansive patterns of thinking are nurtured, where collective aspiration is set free, and where people are continually learning how to learn together'. Senge recommended the use of five 'component technologies' to accomplish these goals: personal mastery, mental models, shared vision, team learning and systems thinking.

Let us look at IIM Kozhikode as a learning organization through this framework:

- Personal mastery is the ability of people to take action and keep learning so that they can keep getting things important to them done. The leaders at IIMK created spaces at the institute to develop and nurture personal mastery. Regular research seminars for knowledge sharing, encouragement and facilitation of faculty and staff in their career progression, enhancement courses, and support of student and alumni initiatives for new learning avenues have empowered the IIMK fraternity to be proactive and keep on learning.
- Mental models describe the presumptions and generalizations people have that influence their actions. The Gurukul,

the circle of contemplation, and the buzz rooms, all very thoughtfully developed at IIMK, nudge people to reflect on their behaviours and beliefs. The meetings convened at these venues are true examples of contemplation in process, where new ideas are acknowledged, thoughts are churned, and the resulting wisdom is transformed into vital decisions.

- Shared vision means all employees in a company share the same vision of where the organization needs to reach. Not only has IIMK been instrumental in carving out a vision for itself and living it through its thoughts, teachings and actions, but it has also played a crucial role in having the vision permeate the endeavours of every stakeholder of the institute. The vision, 'Globalizing Indian Thought', is the breath of the fraternity and finds expression in the programmes offered at the institute as well as in the learning and teaching process here.

- Team learning: When people work well together, they get results that they couldn't have obtained on their own. The institute is known for having foresight into the abilities of people around it and for understanding precisely who will fit into which role and, accordingly, choosing committees (teams) for different tasks. Its belief in the fraternity fills even its rivals with admiration.

- Systems thinking is used to analyse patterns in an organization by looking at it from a holistic viewpoint rather than at its small, unrelated, manageable parts. The institute's enterprise is evident in the way it has led the conception and design of the various units under its wings, letting each unit flourish independently under its overarching vision. IIMK is a strong proponent of strengthening the roots of its tree to ensure that the branches (programmes, centres of excellence, IIMK LIVE, research, consultancy, faculty, staff, students and alumni) are healthy.

Very recently, following my visit to Japan at Suzuki Motor Company, Japan commissioned a research programme on 'Future and Mobility'. In July 2023, I announced the India-Japan Study and Research Centre at IIMK in collaboration with Keio University, a leading private university in Japan. I appointed Prof. Rajib Shaw, a globally renowned disaster management expert, as visiting professor to facilitate India's international relations with Japan.

5

Overcoming Binary Challenges
with Mindfulness

The pure mind is colourless, odourless and tasteless, just like pure water. Pure water acquires the colour of whatever is added to it. Water becomes a bitter cup of coffee or a glass of sweet syrup. A pure mind can, similarly, acquire the colours of its circumstances and become irritable or pleasant. Think of those times when you felt overwhelmed by your circumstances—the frustration you experienced when your flight was cancelled after a long wait at the airport or the agonizing hour you spent outside the emergency ward of a hospital. Think of the bitterness you felt after being backstabbed by a colleague or the surge of pleasure rising up your spine after successfully cracking a tough test.

Circumstances can sometimes affect your body. However, without your permission, no circumstance can affect your mind, whether favourably or adversely. The external world is made up of events and objects. They cannot change your mind without your permission. They require the help of your emotions and predispositions to become coloured. Therefore, face circumstances with the clarity of a pure mind. What colour am I adding to events and objects? This one question can ease you out of many difficult circumstances.

As a leader of institutions, I have had to deal with many binary challenges, most of which had to do with the institutions' journeys from being unknown to well-known. My first stint at IIMK resulted in revolutionary innovations at the institute, while my second has been about setting and meeting ambitious expectations, whether it is the introduction of new programmes or centres of excellence, strengthening IIMK LIVE, or ensuring diversity and inclusion across stakeholders and contexts.

My experience as director general of IMI, Delhi was equally interesting. I was in charge of three campuses: Delhi, Kolkata and Bhubaneshwar. So, my role was to take on a fairly established school and turn it around in such a way that it began to deliver the promise on which it was built. At first, I tried to highlight the international footprint of IMI by strengthening the Indian Technical and Economic Cooperation (ITEC) programme, which brought in a steady stream of participants from several countries to the school. I also recruited some high-quality faculty from across a spectrum of academic areas to enhance the academic life. I spearheaded the rebranding of IMI, transforming it from being perceived merely as a school for a privileged few in Delhi to an esteemed national institution with a global presence. The Association of MBAs (AMBA) granted IMI global accreditation, and IMI began to strengthen its new programmes across all three campuses. My idea was to integrate the three campuses of IMI into one unit so that IMI could serve as a brand. Several faculty members regarded that year and a half at IMI as a steady, innovative, and fruitful period in the institution's history.

Prof. Pinaki Dasgupta, professor at IMI, Delhi, says of my stint there: 'Debashis' people skills, ability to envision things, and, most of all, his ability to create a positive work environment around the place where he is, make him stand apart. When he joined us, IMI was in a quandary and trying to get its mojo back. His first contribution was serendipitous, I guess, when he inculcated the concept of India's first corporate-sponsored business school. Later, he coined the term "boutique business school", and that stuck with us. Gradually, he was able to foster a healthy camaraderie amongst faculty and staff, and every Wednesday he made it a point to get the entire fraternity of staff and faculty together for a cup of tea. That was a simple gesture, but it went many miles to build bridges.'

Group Captain Vivek Dubey (a veteran), registrar and secretary to the BoG and IMI Society, says: 'Debashis, as a trusting boss with a high degree of flexibility and empathy for all stakeholders, won everyone's hearts. His well-known method of blending spiritual principles with modern governance and business norms to achieve excellence and instil ethical practices is truly unparalleled. Grit and determination have always defined Debashis.' IIM Indore faculty member Prof. Venkataraman, a former faculty member at IIMK, too recalls: 'I still remember when IIMK had already built a large auditorium and the older auditorium was being renovated to give it a fresh look. It was a race against time to get the renovated auditorium ready for a major international conference, and Prof. Chatterjee was keeping tabs on the progress being made daily.'

Lakshmi Viswanathan, senior finance and accounts officer at IIMK, says: 'I am a chartered accountant and my core area is working with figures. Whatever I am going to say about Professor Debashis Chatterjee is based on the figures from the financial statements as figures usually tell the truth. His first tenure was from 2008–09 to 2013–14. In those days, the institute was heavily dependent on government grants for its day-to-day running as well as for various campus development expenses. In the 2008–09 fiscal year, the institute had a corpus of approximately Rs 66.47 crore. Today, our corpus is nearly Rs 700 crore. The institute has stopped receiving grants from the government for the past several years. The lion's share of the corpus addition was during the tenure of Prof. Chatterjee. Since his takeover, IIMK has performed in a stellar manner. A director needs to be not only a good academic but also a good administrator. He needs to make the right decisions at the right time and execute them properly. And that's what he did.'

Firstly, it is essential to recognize that higher education does not solely equate to 'hire education'. Instead, the primary focus should be on nurturing our students to become thinkers and innovators, rather than solely pursuing monetary gains. Secondly, the presence of politicians in the realm of higher education often leads to decisions that are politically expedient but academically unsound. It is crucial to prioritize academic integrity over mere political correctness. Thirdly, our approach to education tends to prioritize outcomes over the process of learning. This can be illustrated by the disappointment some parents might feel if their child pursues a different field of study after completing engineering. We need to shift our mindset and place more value on the learning journey itself.

As Indians, we must address our lack of patience for learning and our excessive focus on obtaining degrees as the ultimate goal. True learning requires time and dedication, and we should foster a culture that appreciates and values the process of gaining knowledge. Another significant flaw in our educational institutions is the qualification of teachers without ensuring they possess the necessary quality and expertise. Just as every great individual in history had a guiding mentor, such as Arjuna with Krishna, Chandragupta with Chanakya, and Alexander with Aristotle, we must strive to create exceptional teachers who can inspire and guide students to greatness.

To achieve this, we could consider the establishment of an Indian Teaching Service (ITS) similar to the Indian Administrative Service (IAS). Such a dedicated teaching service would be responsible for nurturing and mentoring educators, ultimately leading to the creation of top-notch learning institutions across the country. By focusing on both students and teachers, we can bring about a positive transformation in our education system.

Management education has been so overrated that business schools have sprouted like seasonal mushrooms. Upon discovery of what their real quality is, campus recruiters and students have gradually withdrawn themselves from these schools. As a result, several schools have either closed down or are on the verge of closure. There is a fine line between an institution's belief in the business of education and education as a business. If an institution looks at education as a business, it is essentially looking for mere profits, and in this case, the institution will be driven by the paradigm of business, which focuses on maximizing profit. The 100 B-schools that have closed down in India probably had to do so because they must not have received the right kind of returns! So, if B-schools say that education is the core and business is the fringe—the way it is at IIMs—closure wouldn't be required. Leadership in a management institution is about overcoming the binaries of excellence and equity; quality and cost; agility of systems and stability of values.

Life is a transit lounge. I am sitting inside the transit lounge of a steel-and-glass airport. I am waiting for my outbound flight. All around me, I see the sleepy faces of fellow 'waiters' reclining on chairs, checking messages, masked up like surgeons in an operation theatre. A noisy kid runs around the lounge, stamping her purple shoes on the marble floor. The lounge cafeteria boy is busy dispensing loud film music with steaming coffee in paper cups. With my bags all checked in, it feels a lot lighter here. I wonder why every phase of life feels somewhat like a wait inside a transit lounge for the next flight.

Waiting to make the next big move.

Waiting to defy gravity for the freedom of the cloudless skies.

Waiting to touch down on the comforting tarmac of Mother Earth.

Waiting is forever, in this interminable terminal called life.

All our wants are followed by waiting.

As a leader of an institution, you must learn to enjoy the wait before wonders happen.

The binary challenges of disbelief in one's capabilities, ego clashes, and being bad mouthed are part and parcel of an academic leader's success story, and I am in no way an exception. However, the art of dealing with roadblocks with grit and determination is something that needs to be imbibed by every leader who aspires to build educational institutions and take them to new heights. My spiritual path facilitated the smoothening of this process.

The two drivers of corporate life are fear and love (FELO). They are like the inhalation and exhalation of corporations. While celebrating the festival of love, we need to understand why fear is a part of love. Corporate minds run on the principle of self-preservation. Looking outwards, captains of industry fear losing out to competitors. Looking within, there are fears about performance appraisals. Then there is the fear of missing out (FOMO) and the fear of having to grovel before an insensitive boss or a complaining customer.

Like the inhale, fear is built on our instinct for survival. However, love is like our out-breath. It is a forward movement from grovelling to growing. It is about voluntarily giving a bit of ourselves to the world. This giving out, or loving, is not transactional, like a well-publicized act of corporate charity or like gifts given to people to manipulate their emotions. True love is like the warmth of a bonfire. It takes nothing back from the hands it has warmed or the hearts it has kindled on a winter's night. It is like a devoted colleague who puts in those inspiring extra hours so that the team can succeed. He seeks no compensation, not even a letter of appreciation for his labour of love. His love for his work is his innate reward. An enduring life and an enduring corporate life are built on the alchemy of opposites: fear and love; control and care; in-breath and out-breath . . .

Love is very important in organizational life. There is more hunger in organizations for love than for bread, butter and incremental jam. People who work around the clock often find themselves extremely lonely. They live in an inner circle of solitary confinement. When two lonely people meet and dislike each other, conflicts arise. Yet, when they begin to appreciate something about the other, the fortress of loneliness is broken and love arises. Love can be expressed through the art of appreciation. Most of us who live in the world of the senses are victims of self-deception. How? The objects that your senses perceive are not isolated at all. They are interconnected time-space events or happenings. Objects in nature are not nouns, but verbs. A tree is 'tree-ing'— growing leaves, shedding them, growing flowers, scattering seeds and 'tree-ing' again. Likewise, your hair is 'hair-ing' and your nails are 'nail-ing'! Interesting, isn't it?

Our worlds are created by categories that pre-exist in the mind in the form of labels. Countries, organizations, markets, products, gender and age are some examples of such labels. Our categorical minds can capture only a deceptively limited world. Yet, we live in a rich and abundant universe, as physicists often tell us. Each fully grown human body has more atoms than there are stars in the visible universe. Our brains have as many neurons as there are stars in a galaxy. Our vision is limited to the spectrum of visible light. We miss the entire orchestra of electromagnetic waves, from radio waves to microwaves; from infrared to ultraviolet light; from X-rays to gamma rays. The path to discovering an abundant world inside of us is a clear and meditative mind.

One of my former students, Amish Tripathi, now a celebrity writer, said, 'The first thing I did when I commenced my career as a writer was to burn my office tie.' That was a symbolic gesture of an upcoming author relinquishing the slavery of corporate life. We wrongly believe that slavery is a thing of the colonial past. In reality, I see many forms of slavery playing out every day in front of me.

Successful people trade away their precious freedom to force themselves to do things against their will. Some suck up to authority, and some flit around like social butterflies in floral dresses and sharp suits to please clients. An expatriate manager slaves and saves money in an alien land to provide for his rainy days. In short, most of us are slaves to something or other. Take stock of the inventory of our slaves: some are slaves of power, others of their positions; some choose to be slaves to technology, while others are slaves to ideology. Most often, slavery is a choice we make. It is for us to decide whether exchanging our freedom for a piece of gold or a garland is worth it!

Our mind is a storehouse of energy pushing against its confines to flow out. This energy feeds on what we let grow in our minds. Do you let garbage grow in your mind? Imagine your feet accidentally stepping on a pile of garbage. What do you do? First, you shrink away. Then you proceed to clean your feet. In short, you try your best to get rid of the garbage. Do you do the same with the mental garbage you consume daily? Consider the fake news, junk entertainment and low-grade information that you allow to be dumped into your mind every day. Do you rent your mind as a storage space for accumulating garbage? Are you mindful of what you see, read or listen to on an everyday basis?

Mindfulness is an occupation without preoccupation. I sort out my mental garbage into two categories: (a) bio-degradable— verbal garbage that degrades naturally in the memory in a day or two; (b) non-biodegradable—conceptual and perceptual garbage that requires years of meditative practice to be even recognized as garbage. One piece of conceptual garbage is 'I am = My Designation'. One is much greater than one is designated to be. Many suffer in the prisons of tags, titles and labels because they can't get this concept clear. One thing I did for my second term as director was to remove my name that's usually stuck along with my designation on the nameplate outside my office. I try to clean out the mental dirt by introspecting, practising mindfulness and using the detergent of positivity and clarity of thought.

Despite living in a corporate ashram, asceticism is not quite my cup of tea. I strive for the middle path between austerity and indulgence. One aspires to live a fine balance of life. Mental equilibrium has been the key to almost every problem that I have encountered and that very balance has kept me sane amid all the insanity around me. We are dedicated to the distribution of bullshit when it comes to ourselves. When we stand before a mirror, we think we are seeing the actual person rather than just a well-dressed, heavily made-up persona we present to the world. In short, we are prone to self-deception, whether we know it or not. Think of the self-assessment exercises that we carry out before performance appraisals. We tend to overestimate our contributions and downgrade our weaknesses and failures to tolerable limits. Our relationship with ourselves is indeed complicated.

Throughout my journey, I've tried to give my all, surpassing the challenges and market downturns I encountered, sometimes outperforming my peers. It's been a path where I rarely sought shortcuts, doing my best to embrace the honest way. I've noticed how frequently we paint aspirational pictures that are yet to come to fruition, concealing our flaws and shortcomings. What if we humbly acknowledged our tendency to deny these fault lines? By doing so, we could become more authentic and integrated human beings, fostering improved relationships with the world around us. Ultimately, this would lead us to evolve into better versions of ourselves.

We are often held hostage by our desires and kidnapped by uncontrollable urges. Our minds can be held to ransom by apparently harmless urges, such as a desire to have an extra scoop of ice cream or another slice of pizza. But many end up regretting their action upon the discovery that pleasure that lasts only a few moments on the lips can end up being a lifelong burden on the hips. An urge arises in our minds, like a small wave, and then it surges to a crest before subsiding on the shore. Surfing the wave of an urge is critical to negotiating our desires. A good surfer rides huge waves successfully with the help of a surfboard. A good way to overcome a million urges in the ocean of our minds is to use conscious breathing as a surfboard. When you are mindful of your incoming and outgoing breaths, you can watch those urges rise and fall without getting traumatized.

While chasing what we deeply desire,
we encounter the anarchy of needless needs.

Happiness comes, not by giving up desires,
but by prioritizing our needs.

Human life serves as a stepping stone, propelling us towards higher states of evolution. It is not a mere haphazard accumulation of experiences. However, many of us tend to behave like scavengers, collecting fragments of experiences throughout our journey from birth to death. Life's true purpose lies in self-discovery, as we learn and reflect upon the reflections in the mirror of our experiences. The ever-evolving human soul consistently questions: who am I beyond these fleeting encounters with images and experiences of life?

Raghuram R. Krishna, co-founder of Genval Consulting Group and a very successful entrepreneur, has this to say: 'Debashis is a humble and high-thinking intellectual who inspires people to take a simplified approach to complex dilemmas faced by industry and government leaders. He aspired to and achieved iconic stardom as one of our foremost thinkers, consistently contributing to the body of management and leadership knowledge with his bestsellers, despite being raised in a humble small-town family in West Bengal.'

Nisha Shukla, who was a participant in the IPMX course in 2014 at IIM Lucknow, says: 'Prof. Chatterjee was the first faculty member to mention mental health, the role of meditation, and how leadership is all about controlling the mind and therefore, thoughts. I remember very vividly that he played soulful music and asked all the participants to close their eyes for ten minutes and just soak in the music. This made the entire class realize how a calm mind breeds ideas and solutions which is a characteristic of an effervescent leader. I feel overwhelmed that Debashis remembered me on his subsequent visit to Pune. When I met him, he exuded the same warmth and greeted me with his charming smile as we made our way to an Italian restaurant for dinner. The next two hours with him was a self-realization journey for me as I heard his thoughts on the varied emotions of a leader. I felt like Siddhartha under the Bodhi tree!'

6

Globalizing Indian Thought

Srikumar Rao is a celebrated best-selling author and elite coach. He has taught at many top business schools in the world and his work has been featured in major media worldwide. Here is what he says about my modest attempt to globalize Indian thought: 'I first met Debashis somewhere around 2007 or 2008 at the Indian School of Business in Hyderabad. I was an invited speaker at a conference on evolving trends in leadership and had flown in from New York. I came out of my room bleary-eyed and jet-lagged, wondering where to go for some food. I met an alert, dapper figure who straightaway recognized me and confessed to being a big fan. We moved together to the dining hall and ate and became friendly. That was Debashis Chatterjee. Humble, friendly, inquisitive and full of joy.

'He did not breathe a word about his many accomplishments or that he was the director of one of the best business schools in

India. I found out about this later. He did talk about his grand vision of leadership and how he planned to improve the diversity record of the IIMs—and Kozhikode in particular—and what he saw as the strengths of management practices in India. Then I discovered we had other interests in common. He was familiar with the philosophical concepts that are India's great gift to the world and saw that these were more relevant than ever to the business environment today. Not just the business environment in India, but globally. Even more important, he was adept at translating those concepts into maxims and management principles and communicating them through stories and case studies. Countless managers have become better leaders as a result of their exposure to Debashis' teaching. As important, they have become better human beings—more peaceful, collected and conscious of the greater good. I am honoured and privileged to have Debashis as a friend and colleague.'

During my interesting conversation with Ramon S. Bhagat Singh, Jr, ambassador of the Philippines to India, he traced his lineage to the Indian freedom fighter Shahid Bhagat Singh. His ancestors from Punjab had migrated to the Philippines and settled there. Ramon Bhagat Singh is a lawyer by profession, and the Philippine president personally chose him to represent his nation in India.

'How do Filipino women and men dominate the space of service providers around the world?' I asked. The smiling ambassador responded by saying that the Philippines has learned to apply the concept of *atithi devo bhava* (the guest is God) from India! I was too stunned to respond when the ambassador presented me with Philippines-made flat samosas and dried mangoes as my takeaways after being communicated some timeless wisdom from India.

'Vision' represents a collection of organizational values that form the basis for an organization's future. It comprises a core ideology and a projected future where these fundamental principles act as the guiding principles. The vision statement of IIMK is 'Globalizing Indian Thought'. The term 'globalization' has always found a place in discussion rounds on the subject of Westernization. But are they synonymous? Indian thought is a major contributor to such discussions. Indian thought, in its varied shades, has been exemplified by icons such as Arjuna, Buddha, Gandhi and Vivekananda. When I took charge of IIMK in 2009, I had a dream—to build the foundation for Globalizing Indian Thought. That dream found a destination on our campus. The Indian Institute of Management, Kozhikode, adopted the mission of globalizing Indian thought a decade ago, and since then it has nurtured it with passion, ideas and enterprise.

The first challenge was to Indianize Indian thought as most educated Indians find our ideas to be alien. Indian thought is an exceptional synthesis of the profound and the profane, of modernity rubbing shoulders with mystery. India is not a succession of hierarchies but rather a conjunction of polar opposite ideas, a sweet synthesis where our many contradictions dissolve. At the pinnacle of material prosperity, we have banked on the power of assimilation and compassion. Indian thought is unique yet embedded in universal human values. Yoga is a transcendental wellness principle and a $65 billion industry today. Our greatest pathfinders and social reformers are our gurus, and they are also our largest global brands.

India does not always need to be the best in the world. India's real challenge is to be 'the best for the world'. Twice as many Indian leaders compared to their US counterparts believe that human capital plays a crucial role in driving successful businesses. This human-centric perspective, which differs from the West's systems-centric view, contributes significantly to our achievements in business. The leaders of India's largest and fastest-growing companies adopt an internal, long-term approach, prioritizing the motivation and development of their employees over short-term shareholder interests. They demonstrate a propensity to consider broader factors, such as public mission and national purpose, beyond the sole focus on stockholder interests.[1]

Indians leap effortlessly from reason to imagination and intuition. This is so evident in the way the narrative plays out in Indian cinema. The hero and the heroine in an Indian movie can break into a song and dance sequence immediately after a car chase or courtroom scene. The material and the mythical coexist in the pan-Indian story. Indian cinema achieves with relative ease what Hollywood spends a fortune to do: a total suspension of disbelief. The audience of Indian cinema just surrenders to the moment, and the magic of our song sequences does indeed work.

Indian managers tend to have a more intuitive grasp of reality, whereas Western-style organizations are based on robust logical analysis and planning. Indian organizations tend to follow an apparently chaotic path. While the West planned its cities before occupying them, Indians first populated a city before planning it. There is an apparent order in the middle of chaos in India. Watch an Indian grocer sell vegetables in a bazaar: he is simultaneously serving five customers, counting money, watching weights,

Wearing my first suit during my kindergarten days

Bitten by the writing bug—typing out an article in my Periyar hostel room no. 101,
Jawaharlal Nehru University

TEDx talk at Indian Management Institute, Delhi

Conversation with Amitabh Kant, chief executive officer of Niti Aayog as director-general of IMI, Delhi

Talking about education with the Dalai Lama

Inaugurating new batch of PGP students

The idea of globalizing Indian thought has been widely covered by the media

Chief of the navy staff, Admiral Karambir Singh in Visakhapatnam, with whom we discussed the art of war and the Bhagavad Gita

From satori to samadhi: globalizing Indian thought. In conversation with Francesc Miralles, the bestselling author of *Ikigai* in my Gurukul

Typical leadership retreat in the Gurukul classroom commissioned in 2021

With Duvvuri Subbarao, former Reserve
Bank of India governor on IIMK campus

With my former student and popular
writer, Amish Tripathi

Reminiscence of singer KK at IIMK just a month before he passed away

With the inimitable Shashi Tharoor

With two iconic personalities, former president Pranab Mukherjee and former Puducherry lieutenant governor Kiran Bedi in Delhi

Our little joint family: (from left to right) Aditi, Mig, Shrishti and Siddharth (picture taken a few months before Mig passed away peacefully in 2022)

bargaining with a customer, and keeping an eye on potential theft . . . all of these in a sweeping, intuitive grasp.

Think of the Kumbh Mela, which takes place every twelve years at the confluence of three rivers (one which is now extinct) in northern India. Touted as the largest gathering on earth, about 100 million people make their way through structures that are temporarily created and removed once the *mela* is over. This densely packed mobile crowd is larger than the population of most countries in the world. Yet, a seemingly noisy and unruly ocean of human beings finds order in chaos. Traffic managers slow the movement of people as they walk to the confluence and back in long queues. By default, perfect strangers in the human system slow each other down. While the corporate world across the globe believes in the credo of 'the faster the better', India often demonstrates that slower is sustainable.

Here is India's management mantra that the West can pick up from the *Kumbh Mela*: to civilize is to collaborate; to collaborate is to civilize. When 100 million people learn to collaborate for a shared purpose, a mammoth organization of humanity takes shape. A pot-bellied billionaire moves alongside a naked sadhu; a gang of villagers files past a conference of dozing cows; romance blooms; pockets are picked—yet almost everyone gets home safely at the end of the pilgrimage!

Purpose and meaning are of utmost importance in life. For some, purpose means to be successful; for some, it is to be rich; for others, it is to attain milestone after milestone; and for still others, there is no target to attain.

I have been in the pursuit of globalizing Indian thought. My work to reach this goal was clear in everything I did in the institutions I could manage to serve with my vision. For nearly three decades, I have attempted to interpret Indian thought for the world. My purpose is to establish Indian management wisdom as one of the greatest soft-power assets of our country. I am happy to be able to interpret India and Indian wisdom for the larger world. In short, that is my purpose.

It was about twenty-five years ago that the seed of this idea sprouted in my mind: what is Indian about the Indian Institute of Management? That seed has emerged as IIMK's institutional pursuit. The purpose is the art of assimilating many goals. Everything in nature is driven by a larger purpose. Look at a spider's web and its intricate artistry—the spider's nervous system is primitive, but with the help of its ecology the spider can execute textile engineering of great sophistication in the form of its web. A beehive is an extraordinary piece of civil engineering. The hexagonal walls of the hive are inclined at a certain angle so that the honey does not run out and the temperature of the hive is kept constant. A monarch butterfly and its family have extraordinary navigation skills. They begin their migration from the Amazon forest in South America, reach Canada, and come back to the same Amazon forest after several generations. How do they do this? Generations of monarch butterflies live with the shared purpose of returning to their origins. The spider, bee, or butterfly may have rudimentary nervous systems, but their intent is pure. Therefore, they can accomplish what they do through their larger environment.

I once met the Cuban ambassador to India, Alejandro Simancas Marin, when he was newly appointed. The links between Cuba and India go back to the visits of the Cuban leader Fidel Castro and the iconic Che Guevara to India. Both had a deep admiration for Mahatma Gandhi. Ambassador Alejandro Marin presented me with a Cuban cigar. He said the cigar was more than just addictive entertainment. In Cuba, the cigar is believed to ward off mosquitoes, insects and evil spirits. I told him that India has a similar custom of using the fragrant smoke of *agarbattis* to ward off mosquitoes and insects. Just that we don't smoke agarbattis! India adapted to growing and eating chilli from South Americans and drinking tea from the British. Indian culture is driven by a purposive intent— assimilation and adaptation.

Management is India's most successful soft power. Most people in our country do not realize that. We have sent our managers out into the world, and they are now in charge of companies such as IBM, Microsoft and Google. What makes it possible for our managers to do so well globally? It is the deep orientation of values in India that makes wealth creation sacred and legitimate. One way to express India's soft power is to provide management education that is deeply rooted in not just the symbolism but the actuality of what it means for one to be an Indian. We want to maximize India's clout and impact in the world and reclaim our thought leadership.

One big idea is that India will have to find its own trajectory towards making a global impact. India's core ethos has been *vasudhaiva kutumbakam*, the universe of borderless humanism. India's mantra of borderless humanism will have a far-reaching impact on India's rise as a global force. From our old obsession with non-alignment, India has moved to multi-alignment. A culture of genuine multilateralism is reflective of India's spirit of harmony, assimilation and adaptation.

Indian thought comes from the depth of the spirit and breath of a syncretic culture. People have been in awe of it, and scholars have frequently found its strangeness and uniqueness to be intriguing. While some have explored Indian thought through yoga, some from across the globe have drawn inspiration from it.

I am reminded of a conversation I had with a naval commander in Australia who said that he thought India was among the richest countries in the world, and added, 'Imagine that the unit of currency of a nation is not the rupee, dollar, pound or yen—but a human being!' This made me realize that India was already a billionaire country and was growing every day! What a non-conventional way of looking at India's population, which we have grown up thinking of as a problem. Now, you see, our huge population is like a real wealth-creating opportunity for the country. The ability to create wealth is more precious than having wealth.

Indian thought has always intrigued me and led me to have faith in its ethos. A vast body of literature has risen from this glorious land, despite destruction by invaders. The writings of stalwarts, from Rabindranath Tagore to Kabir, have always given me food for thought. Their eloquence, their choice of words and the hope in their voices mesmerize those who have had the privilege to read them.

Tagore said, 'If India can find a solution to her problems, it will be a solution for all humanity.' The question is: can Indians truly come together with a unity of purpose? Luckily, in a world of competing modernity and fractured identities, India still holds its own. At no point in history has one-sixth of humanity cohesively formed a single political entity, despite every disruptive force that has acted on it for thousands of years. Our moment has now come! We have enough quality managers, engineers and doctors. Where indeed have the dreamers gone?

Our vision for IIM Kozhikode is to 'Globalize Indian Thought'. It is important to understand how, in the business school culture, where most ideas and theories are drawn from the Western world, IIM Kozhikode has chosen to chase a different dream.

The institute has been working consistently on this vision. The richness of India, with its heritage, traditions, wisdom and thoughts, draws us to believe that this is possible. Globalization is much more than Westernization. Indigenous practices like the *dhandha* and *langar* systems, amongst others, which were born in India, have already been discussed widely. And here is IIMK, playing its role in the emergence of an India that is altogether new. It started the Indian Business Museum on campus with the thought of creating a storehouse of knowledge about the country's business heritage for keen business minds interested in the roots of Indian business. The aim was to make the business history of India a topic of discussion across the world, which has so far been dominated by Western analytical thought.

The very concept of a business museum was somewhat novel for Indian management education. The limelight turned on the institute once again when it conceptualized and orchestrated its execution, the result of which was an astonishing piece of work, a unique creation. And was the Indian Business Museum enough to globalize Indian thought?

Yes, when we were establishing it, we said there is no museum of this kind in the country that showcases the journey of Indian business. As you can see, it also has to do to do with Kerala and its ethos. We said that the IIM in Kerala should reflect the features and excellence of the. I learned that in 1498, Kozhikode was the first modern city in India. It was the starting point of urbanization in India. We decided to showcase that in the museum and show how Indian business, trade and industry evolved.

Apart from the Indian Business Museum, many other constituents of the campus embody the very essence of Indian-ness. The Arjuna statue, standing tall in the main block of the institute, is the personification of Dharma, an ethical code for every ancient Indian hero in everything he or she did. The institute buildings are named after well-known characters from Indian history, culture or mythology, like Kautilya and Viveka, or after ancient universities like Nalanda and Takshshila. Classroom clusters carry the names of Indian icons such as Aryabhatta, Bheem, Karna and Kabir. Along with the statues of Vivekananda and Buddha, you will find insights from the masters, such as Tagore and Mother Teresa. The institute teaches business in a place where the students get soaked in the rain of Indian music, which echoes in our curious minds. Its belief in the Indian thought system is the essence of IIMK's existence. Indianness is reflected not just in our physical infrastructure but also in the way we dream, we think and the understated pride in our ethos.

'From IIMK, Debashis invited me to a workshop on "How to Remain Relevant in Academia" for his faculty members in 2012, and to another workshop on "Research Methods for Doctoral Students" in 2013. During these visits, I came to understand Debashis's goal—to transform IIMK from a relatively unknown national institution to one of international repute during his five-year term. The inspiring quotes displayed across the campus, including in the upcoming children's park, showed that he was committed to making things happen at IIMK. The invitation for my lecture at the Pan-IIM World Management Conference in 2014 gave me yet another opportunity to understand and appreciate what Debashis had already achieved as director of IIMK. Of his several notable achievements, the insightfully constructed Indian Business Museum and Management Development Centre caught my attention,' says Prof. Ramadhar Singh, former professor at the National University of Singapore and a globally acclaimed scholar.

At a time when the programme curriculum continued to be age-old across schools offering management education, we made waves when we introduced, with foresight, the humanities and liberal arts in the management area. It raised many an eyebrow because these subjects were not considered to be crossing paths with management in any way. We taught courses based on classics as well as Gandhian leadership. As a leap forward, IIMK conceptualized and successfully delivered a unique offering in the form of a full-time MBA in liberal studies and management.

When you look at the complexity of problems that managers are going to be required to solve in the future, compounded by climate change, terrorism, and other foreseen and unforeseen calamities, management graduates will require a broad range of thinking skills and awareness of the world. They should be able to extract actionable insight from a sea of data in an uncertain environment. This will be the most important managerial skill required. I am proud to share that IIM Kozhikode is the only B-school in the nation that boasts of the co-existence of the dynamic humanities and liberal arts with the core business disciplines such as operations management, marketing and finance in the management area. This area houses vibrant courses like social transformation in India and business history on the one hand, and communication and narratives of wisdom on the other. We pioneered the two-year full-time MBA in liberal studies and management, which is now the dream of many other leading educational institutes.

Aparajith Ramnath, an Oxford scholar and former faculty member at IIMK, says, 'As a historian, I greatly appreciated the efforts Professor Chatterjee has been making to integrate the teaching of the humanities into management education. An exciting museum of Indian business had been set up on campus, and there was strong support for the inclusion of business history in the curriculum. There was a sense of possibility, and the students were excited by the new offerings. That there is a strong desire among students to explore the insights offered by the liberal arts is apparent once more from the response to the recently launched liberal studies in management programme.'

I wonder how we can bring together tales from the Mahabharata and apply them to the drama and politics that go on inside corporate boardrooms. Have you ever wondered why only Hercules, Achilles, and their ilk are remembered across the world when we talk of some of the greatest mythological characters and not Arjuna or Krishna from the Indian epics? I, in my capacity as a human being, nurtured by tales from our rich heritage, would wish that heroic Indian mythological tales are remembered by mankind. Isn't that a legitimate thing to aspire to?

One of my favourite students, Ishant Saxena, a globetrotter and CEO of a large pharmaceutical company writes in his reminiscences: 'Dr Chatterjee and I go back many years. When he was a teacher at my alma mater, IIM Lucknow, we were all impressed by his erudition, gravitas and perspective. He talked of things which were central to everyone's lives and provided philosophical insights. His lectures—quoting from mythologies and other important texts—were an absolute treat. He was also a strict academician—once I missed his class to attend my then-girlfriend's birthday (now my wife!) and saw my grades reduced by half!

'Very few Indian professors had a desire to propagate their knowledge in popular media, but Prof Debashis was different—he wrote dozens of books and regular columns in the *Times of India*. He also had a global outlook—studying as a Fulbright scholar in the US, teaching at Harvard and running a business school in Singapore—again, rare for most Indian professors.

'Later, our paths crossed again when he recommended me to the board of IIM Amritsar, one of the newer IIMs and it was an honour to work together in the initial institution building. My daughter wrote her first book and Prof. Debashis was gracious enough to write a blurb.

'Thank you professor for the time together.'

7

The Art and Practice of Leadership

Leadership in academic institutions involves inculcating certain traits. These traits encompass safeguarding the school's autonomy, actively involving academics in crucial decision-making, fostering collegiality through democratic processes and cooperation, and advocating for the school's interests when dealing with senior administrators. Academics tend to favour leaders who employ subtle leadership rather than resorting to overt autocracy. The application of minimal leadership not only offers faculty autonomy and support but also contributes to enhancing the school's credibility and reputation. One can liken such a leader to an orchestra conductor, guiding and harmonizing the efforts of the team towards success. You have to be involved yet detached from the field of execution.

Leadership of schools does not adhere to a single, rigid definition. Instead, it has evolved to encompass various perspectives, including individual leader attributes and styles, as well as broader process and relational approaches that involve both leaders and their followers. I believe that the leadership process entails three distinct types of responsibilities. Firstly, there is the institutional leadership process, which involves setting the school's direction and strategic objectives while fostering a sense of unity and shared values among its members. Secondly, the social leadership process comes into play, focusing on strategic transformation, execution, and implementation, particularly to inspire, mobilize, assist, and empower the school's faculty and staff. Lastly, the structural leadership process takes charge of directing the organization through effective planning, control and organizational design. Importantly, there exist strong systemic and feedback connections between strategic intent, strategic implementation and execution, and strategic planning and control. As a result, these three leadership processes are not mutually incompatible but rather work in harmony to propel the organization forward. Think of the ignition, accelerator and brakes of a car. Ignition is strategic intent, the accelerator is tactical speed and the brakes provide an institutional control system.

From the standpoint of leadership and governance, it is crucial for an academic leader to effectively mould three critical and essential components in the process of building a business school's values, purposes and positions. These components are the academic model, the economic model and the strategic agenda. The academic model describes the nature and form of the research activities and instructional aims pursued by the academic institution. A decision may need to be made regarding maintaining a healthy balance between the engagement of corporations and academics. The economic model addresses the question of how the institution will be able to create the necessary monetary resources to maintain its levels of research, teaching and community engagement. The strategic agenda provides a framework that attempts to integrate academic strategic activities with the resources offered by the various economic and business models. Therefore, the responsibility of academic leaders is to champion the leadership processes of their respective schools and to manage, construct and carry out the strategic agenda of their respective schools over time.

Problem Comprehension

Understanding the environmental and competitive backdrop is crucial for determining tactical prospects and finding strategies to align those activities with the organizational and political framework of the school. These activities or projects should be presented and explained in a way that encourages both potential supporters and detractors to express their opinions and participate in an open discussion regarding their viability. This desire for more openness, unity and connection also manifests as an expression of respect and trust for other people. New ideas and tactical alternatives may be developed when people are urged to be more open, invited to 'think outside the box' and made to feel 'comfortable' sharing their viewpoints. People will then sense that their strategic aptitude is more highly valued. As a result, it is crucial to look at both the 'what' and the 'how' of a leader. Researchers shed light on the concept of 'primal leadership' and the importance of emotional intelligence (EI).

Creating an atmosphere of trust and resonance is key, as it allows leaders to bring out the best in their team members. This holistic approach to leadership empowers leaders to free the potential of every individual, leading to better outcomes for the entire school community.

Problem Diagnosis

The importance of possible strategic issues should be continuously evaluated by the academic leaders, but they should also consider the effort necessary to 'legitimize' these challenges, particularly in securing faculty and board support. While some strategic concerns may require a significant, radical change or breakthrough in the school's current plan, others may proceed more logically and gradually. Radical transformation frequently necessitates a stretched approach and extensive organizational adaptability.

Problem Legitimization

Extensive legitimization efforts are typically required for breakthrough issues and methods. Academic leaders may forget to include alternative opinions and improvements in conceptualizing strategic goals when they are driven to work tirelessly to implement their vision and ideas. Although a commanding leadership style is typically required to spearhead breakthrough efforts, it should be accompanied by unambiguous communication as well as a desire to listen to and learn from key constituencies' opinions and discussions. While attempting to institutionalize the idea of globalizing Indian thought, I recognize how critical it was to clearly communicate the vision and action choices of staff and faculty.

Power Activation

In the end, it is the leaders' responsibility to utilize their authority to move those initiatives forward by enlisting the participation of key decision-makers. Therefore, leadership can be defined as a process of political and social influence in which leaders make it their mission to comprehend the perspectives and motivations of those around them, combining this knowledge with the point of view of actors representing various institutions to determine the most effective next step. Consequently, academic leaders are required to make use of their power to bring the leadership process to a conclusion. They must successfully rally support and commitment to successfully promote and carry out any plan. The influence of the academic leader in hierarchical, professional institutions like business schools is contingent on the individual's expertise, trustworthiness, professional reputation, personal prestige, capacity to deliver results, honesty, commitment, interpersonal skills and other characteristics. It is highly challenging for academic leaders to make use of the positional power that comes with their job unless they have already demonstrated their value, courage, and success in a variety of earlier decision opportunities—in other words, unless they have a substantial track record. I was lucky to have a track record as the dean of an international business school in Singapore before I took on the role of director at IIMK.

Leaders are accountable for determining the course their institution will take. In fact, their duty is to mould strategy for their institution and make it function in such a way that daring breakthrough projects can be pursued and successfully carried out when necessary. We launched four new post-graduate programmes between 2020 and 2021 with a clear intent to see them deliver the intended outcomes.

In analysing the components of this paradigm, Henry Mintzberg's image of the academic leader's style as the 'orchestral conductor' is crucial. As an imaginative and perceptive organizer and coordinator, an academic leader must have and use a variety of personal traits. To handle a variety of jobs, such as those of strategist, implementer, human-capital developer and talent manager, the traits required would include self-awareness, confidence, motivation, empathy, social skills and intuition. The leader must be able to establish the business school's broad, strategic objective, foster trust and provide answers to questions like 'what are we doing?' Additionally, it is crucial to identify the school's core competencies and give teachers, students and the university a clear direction in terms of the speed, ease and brand development required to successfully implement the school's strategy.

Leadership is not the same as sales. One needs to delegate, train and multiply, and if one doesn't do that, one will stagnate. Very often, we get trapped in a web of aspirations and set ambitious goals for ourselves and our teams. The world is evolving, but has the definition of leadership maintained pace with the fast-evolving world? Are we still discussing leadership in terms of charisma, likeability index, behavioural traits, styles and acceptance? Is it really possible to compartmentalize leaders as democratic, autocratic, laissez-faire, servant, authentic, progressive, and so on?

Aren't leaders more than their styles and their approaches? Do leaders control or manage situations and emotions?

I have always been a strong believer in developing one's individual leadership model rather than idolizing any existing framework. It is when one is able to discover and liberate one self from the limits of definitions and theories that one succeeds in crafting one's personal touch to leadership, which is authentic—no imitation, involving no adaptation, no acting. Only being one's true self.

Let go of a few of your many yearnings. Think of the monkey with a handful of peanuts trying to free its hand trapped inside a glass jar. All the monkey needs to do to be free is drop a few nuts.

When our yearnings exceed our earnings, we need to pause, reflect and let go of a few of them to excel in life. When I landed in Kunnamangalam, then a small village near Kozhikode, from Singapore sometime in 2009 to interview for the post of IIM Kozhikode's director, the chairperson of the selection board, E. Sreedharan, India's metro man, asked me whether I had been told that I was too young for the leadership post. I was just in my early forties at the time. I told the interview board that you don't grant leadership, you just grant a position. How can you grant someone leadership? You can give me a role, but leadership is what I have to earn.

In my three terms, spanning from April 2009 to September 2014 and from June 2018 to date, I happen to be the longest-serving director of IIMK, which has completed its twenty-seventh year of existence. I am humbled to have played a part in seeing the transformation of this management institute from its humble beginnings in an obscure town to its current position among the top seventy-five in the world. Our success is attributed to the collective efforts of a dedicated team and numerous innovative initiatives that we have undertaken along the way.

I have often shared the story objectively of when I attended the interview for the post of director at IIMK. I was put up in a guesthouse where the kettle did not work, the sofa creaked and the door didn't close. When I was asked what I would do if I were appointed the director of IIMK, I candidly said that if I were to come back and take the role of the director, I would sort out things that were not working, including people.

I knew that when one inherits an institution, one does not inherit a lot of buildings or infrastructure. One inherits a lot of conversations. IIMK's challenges back then were connectivity, size and location. We beat these by going digital in 2001. Most of our institutional decisions came from the pursuit of a larger purpose under the leadership of Prof. Kalro. I completely subscribed to the fact that if there is no purpose, there is no leadership. I was given a role, and leadership is what I earned.

I know that people seek pleasure and security and a leader is seen as the person who can help them achieve that. More than a compelling vision or goal, the possibility of achieving one or both of the aforesaid goals makes people follow a leader. Leadership is a much-debated subject and a badly bruised one too; a million theories and experts push and shove to be seen and heard. Let me simplify leadership by describing the four important qualities of a leader:

1. Authenticity
2. Productivity
3. Connectivity
4. Possibility

Authenticity

A leader gets the trust of his followers by displaying this trait. Do what needs to be done—a leader needs to display this in word and deed. Being human, being humble and getting rid of the ego are essential supporting factors for this trait.

I was attending a high-profile wedding in Bengaluru. After the ceremony, everyone got in line to greet the newlyweds, and I joined the queue with the others. Slowly the thrill of attending a big wedding was replaced with irritation. Why did I have to stand in a queue to meet the couple? It was then that I turned around to check who else was enduring the same suffering. Around ten positions behind me, Azim Premji was waiting patiently, and a few places behind him was Kiran Majumdar Shaw. I saw a broad smile on his face, and my irritation and ego just evaporated at that moment.

It was a great example of leadership in action—those industry leaders could have taken the easy route; no one in the room would have complained if they'd broken the queue and walked up to greet the couple, but they did not. Transformation will happen at the rate of reality—can you remove all the show and hype and tell it to the people as it is? It makes you more believable and worth following.

Productivity

Productivity is potential minus interference. We are talented and have immense potential to be the best in our chosen professions, but we are rarely willing to do what it takes to be the best. Most people want achievement and success without effort. So we fall by the wayside and become also-rans. The best leaders do what is needed; they make sacrifices, stick to the task, and reap the rewards for doing so. As leaders, we need to unleash the potential of our team—a leader is only as good as his team; when the team achieves glory, he does too.

Procrastination is a major reason for failure or our inability to achieve our true potential. We allow things to pile up because we are waiting for a good day. Big achievers are not those who do things in bursts, but rather, they just keep doing things in reasonable amounts and regularly. If we plan to cover a distance of 1000 kilometres on foot, the best way to do it would be to cover 15–20 kilometres a day and just keep doing that. The kind who say that they will wait for the right weather and then do 50–60 kilometres in one stretch will never get there.

Be consistent and keep doing your quota. This can be illustrated with a personal example: despite having written more than seventeen books and being a widely published author, there was a time when I had not written anything in spite of wanting to do so. I had been waiting for the right day because there were a million other things to do. Then I hit upon this plan to write 500 words every day, before breakfast. My mantra, 'No 500 words, no breakfast' really worked. No matter what else was planned, I would get this task completed on most days, and that is how I removed all the (self-made) roadblocks and harnessed my potential to the optimum.

Connectivity

This is about seeing how the various parts are connected to the whole—like how the blind men in the fables help each other visualize an elephant. It is also about connecting with the people around us—networking and associating. A true leader has her finger on the pulse of her followers and a complete understanding of the environment in which she operates.

Disengaging with followers or associates can be dangerous. Research has shown that by ignoring people, a leader can be as much as 40 per cent disengaged from the people around him. He will not get critical information because the channels of communication are shut, and he will lose influence and trust. Although I do not recommend it, I am in favour of even criticizing people as better than disengagement—while criticizing you are still in touch, which reduces the level of disengagement.

But the best way to reduce or remove disengagement is to appreciate and recognize people. When appreciated or valued, employees engage strongly with the leadership. So, it is important to focus on the positives. Believe in the possible! Moreover, leaders should stop passing judgements and stick to the realm of reality. Operate with facts and data, and you will rarely go wrong. It is also advantageous to check how one is viewed by others. Leaders can modify their behaviours and their mode of engagement with their followers by being aware of what their followers think about them. I prefer to be known as 'an avid learner' because of my belief that every human being is a work in progress till eternity.

Possibility

I have come to realize that all possibilities in life exist in the space between two thoughts. This space may be described as the field of being—simply being with full awareness.

You may like to hear what Tarun Raj, a former PGDM student at IIM Lucknow, has to say: 'I still remember the organizational behaviour class taken by Prof. Debashis Chatterjee, popularly known as Deb Chat, on leadership way back in 2002 at IIM Lucknow: "You need not wait for the organization to give you a role, you can carve out one for yourself." In our class, 'values in action in our education system', we had to survey fifteen schools and 700+ kids across eleven cities. Despite several challenges, Deb Chat's encouragement motivated us. We were covered in a national newspaper and also published a monograph. For me, the impact of his words went beyond that project. For the final placement, I aimed for HR despite companies not visiting our college for HR roles. Through negotiation, I secured an HR job, which I consider one of my best decisions. While I may have earned less, I find satisfaction in my work. I owe a lot to him.'

Much of my innovation as a leader came from the field of possibility. Leaders are often hemmed in by mental models— thought structures borrowed from the past. I meditate every morning and evening on my breath and find a way to slip into the space of immense possibilities between thoughts. This is where most of my creative ideas and action choices come from.

To achieve and practise leadership, one must utilize different tools and perspectives to tackle the different challenges that come one's way. Like an artist uses different brushes to create his piece of art, I use different approaches through which I can demonstrate a different way of looking at a problem. I think leaders don't do more; they see more and become aware of opportunities hiding inside a problem and this is why they can solve problems that others cannot. Hence, leadership is about perspective as well as execution, because if you simply wish to execute, you might as well be a mechanic. Leadership is about mobilizing the energy of a large number of people towards the right perspective.

IIMK trains students to become better managers. Many people enter the workplace with a certain image of themselves, which is very detrimental to their growth. They come with a chip on their shoulder as managers, but because they are working for the first time they do not have access to the tools of the organization to influence people. Hence, one's ability to influence people will depend a lot on one's personal qualities. Your influence must be greater than your formal authority for you to be a leader. On the IIM campus, students learn that aspiration is more valuable than resources.

Knowledge is power, but the right attitude would be a more powerful tool to have. Students learn that a synergistic way of doing things is way better than being a lonely wolf on the prowl. Not everyone is designated as a leader, and you don't need to be born a leader. You are born with certain qualities pertaining to the art of leadership. This is what is exemplified at the IIM campus. These dormant qualities of the head and heart are amplified by peer groups, teachers and others. I introduced the idea of a treasure hunt as part of our induction process for the upcoming MBA class of 2023. At the end of it, I told them that the real treasure is between your ears.

Leaders have a deep reservoir of energy. If one can acquire this depth of vitality, it will take one very far in life. Slight knowledge of a book and scoring good marks in examinations are not enough to make someone a leader. What makes someone a leader is the ability to unleash one's energy to inspire and move people. The ability to inculcate such qualities in others is the role of a coach. We call ourselves management schools and not business schools because a much broader spectrum of knowledge is distributed here. With this knowledge, our students run multidisciplinary businesses and other kinds of enterprises. Thus, you could say that our students grow roots in the ground as well as develop wings to fly.

I completely agree that a leader's efforts are all the more crucial when the economy is down, especially when it is not going to open up at the same level as before. There are two aspects to working in such an economy. One is your own capability. The second, and not so well-known aspect, is your ability to cope with difficulties. This is very crucial for everyone, from business leaders to students. How we can cope with dwindling expectations and how we can cope with decreasing customer interest are the two questions that will need answers. The only salvation for an enterprise in a market that is dead is to re-invent itself. I still remember the story of Konosuke Matsushita of the Panasonic company. Due to a crisis in the Japanese economy, his company was in the dumps. He had two options. One was to sell the company, and the other was to pay his employees half their salaries and ask them to turn it around within six months. He offered them ownership of the company if they could do so, because he was going to sell it anyway. For six months, the employees worked so energetically that they completely transformed the company. As promised, Matsushita gave the company to them. When a journalist asked him why he did so, he replied that he simply held out an umbrella to his employees when it was raining.

When I joined as director, IIM Kozhikode was facing a crisis of losing faculty to other institutes. We were geographically isolated but soon we bounced back because our team of faculty became more innovative in that situation. The educational sector will move more towards the educational-technological sector. Hence, there will be sunrises and sunsets. One has to look for new possibilities. A lot of people fail to spot an opportunity when it arises. People should develop the habit of seeing the big picture in small pictures. We need to have that big picture in mind because there is still hope. I use the analogy of a cup of tea, wherein I tell them that they are drinking photons—the photons that have fallen on the tea leaves, which we dry till they become brown so that we can use them. But we don't consume them dry; we put them in water and boil them. If this does not yield the desired taste, we add white milk from a good cow that grazes on a green field. To improve the taste further, we add crystallized sap from the sugarcane grown on earth. All these elements of life are compiled into one cup of tea. This is the big picture of a cup of tea: air, water, fire and earth coming together in a cosmic conspiracy to make it.

One of the most prominent leadership qualities I believe in is that a leader not only grows within a culture but also carries a culture within himself. When you practise using elements of your cultural attribute and become proficient enough that they will become second nature to you, that is when you will find that transformation has already occurred. *Darshan* is vision—sight and insight. *Swadhya* is the reflection of self-study. *Sahayog* is teamwork. *Sthiapragnya* is equanimity of mind. *Purnatwa* is the state of being fulfilled. These are the five facets of leadership from the classical Indian wisdom leadership manual.

It is extremely important that our leaders lead with wisdom and credibility. People's trust in a leader adds to the leader's credibility only when it is not blind trust. Therefore, a leader followed by sheep will produce toxic leadership. There is one Buddha and a billion *buddhus* (fools)! One visionary and a million cataract patients. One baba, followed by a resounding baa! Baa! Some of them turned out to be the proverbial black sheep. The Baba's followers rioted, and some were tragically killed even as he was being convicted for heinous crimes. The fury of his followers was matched only by the depth of their delusion. We witnessed how millions of people can outsource their aspirations, fantasies and anxieties to a socially constructed god.

The sheep that do not use their God-given intelligence are bound to be led away by clever foxes. Organizations led by toxic bosses produce cultures of defensiveness and secrecy. You can call them organizational foxholes. Inside these foxholes, the followers bury their antipathy, anger and discontent. This makes the organization a minefield that is destined to go up in flames someday. Toxic bosses are those who suck the energy and vitality out of organizations, like vampires. While leaders mobilize energy within an organization for a greater purpose, toxic bosses mortgage organizational energy to promote themselves.

Bosses operate from their ego centres, and this leads to three distinct behaviours: arrogance, bitchiness and cowardice.

Arrogance: Arrogant bosses let flattery go to their heads and fear of failure sink into their hearts. They claim organizational successes as their own. You can see arrogance in their exaggerated gestures, in the falsity of their claims, in the glare of their gaze and their relentless chest-thumping. Soon, however, the arrogance of incumbency will encounter the ambush of insurgency. The more arrogant the incumbent, the more deviant the insurgent.

Behind a toxic boss is often a traumatic childhood. Behind an anxious managing director is often an insecure mother-in-law. In organizations led by arrogant autocrats, anger and protest go underground—deep inside foxholes. Feedback channels are clogged like choked pipelines. Discussion about the boss through winks and nudges goes on inside staff canteens and around tea dispensers. Employees are just one alcoholic drink away from letting you know what they think of their bosses.

Bitchiness: This is a trait that is gender-neutral. You can have a bitchy boss perpetually breathing down your neck to micromanage every activity of yours. 'So, you had a beard trim during office hours?' He might growl. 'Doesn't my beard grow during office hours?' You might argue. But that argument is unlikely to douse the heat of his bitchiness. He will soon catch you distracted by Facebook while on company time. Then the boss shoots off a memo describing you as a distracted but satisfactory underperformer. Bitchiness in a boss is the sadistic psychological itch that keeps the team on tenterhooks.

Cowardice: Fear rules organizational foxholes. Bosses are just too scared to take bold decisions. They hide behind power games, precedent and prejudice. There is no such thing as an honest coward. For a cowardly boss, fear wears a mask called pragmatism. Cowardice is always a cover for deep insecurities and insincerities within the boss's psyche.

Like a dancing Nataraja, but quite the opposite of the dynamism of the image, the cowardly boss clutches onto his chair with his left hand and mildly shakes others' chairs with his right. Cowardice gives rise to something designed to project the exact opposite: bragging. The boss loves to be seen as larger than life— at least in the adulating gaze of his subjects. As in the episode of the Ba! Ba! Black Sheep who pulled the wool over our eyes, this syndrome is everywhere for us to see: in business, in politics, in schools, and in the fields of entertainment and sports.

A leader is no better than a solitary, still frame. However, leadership is like an engaging, energizing movie. A movie is much more than a sum of still frames. The movie of leadership involves a dynamic interplay of energy between a leader and his followers. The minefield called the organization becomes a dance floor when leaders stop behaving like toxic bosses. An inspired and responsible leader then becomes the choreographer of the dance of possibilities, like a true Nataraja. She mobilizes extraordinary energy within herself and in her followers. This is the energy of shared purpose. An organization that has found a common purpose kisses the sky with effortless ease—like a flock of geese! When you drop out of your ego centre, you drop into a large universe of possibilities. Your world transforms as your perception shifts.

One of the most difficult tasks in leadership is to be able to face facts and see them for what they are without reacting. If someone is criticizing you upfront or even behind your back, don't jump to conclusions about his or her motives. They may just be trying to express their displeasure at your actions rather than harm you. Attend to your first raw impressions rather than to the first or immediate interpretation of someone's motives. Be as objective as possible; you can never be fully objective but still try to work past your biases. Don't add to the facts the spicy self-talk—the interpretative stuff—going on inside your head. You will be happier about it.

When brands become leaders, it is imperative for them to also become icons of trust. Jaguar Land Rover's marketing director, Anthony Bradbury says, 'What matters most for our brand are absolute transparency, complete focus, and the informal breaking down of silos.' Have you ever wondered why McDonald's advertises its supply chain rather than its burgers? It is to earn the trust of its customers by increasing internal visibility so that consumers can track the end-to-end processes that go into the making of a burger.

Branding is the art, craft and science of achieving consistency of values in an inconsistent world. The science of branding involves tracking the performance of a brand. The art of branding has to do with creating stories that move and mesmerize customers. The craft of branding is about delivering brand performance day after day. At IIM Kozhikode, I see my role as a trustee and a servant of an educational brand that stands for our three stated values: authenticity, sustainability and fulfilment—*satyam, nityam* and *purnam*.

Satya Nadella, CEO of Microsoft, says, 'In redefining fulfilment, what I'm trying to do is harmonize what I deeply care about, my deep interests, with my work.' Personal motivation is not the same as organizational motivation. Organizations tend to standardize human motivators such as money or power in the form of generalized performance structures measured against time. On the other hand, at the personal level, human beings get motivated in a million different ways by different things in different time frames. If you wish to find out what motivates you, look for those little micro-inspirational moments that you experience when performing a complex, challenging task. These little micro-inspirations will give you clues as to what fulfils you! Some say leaders are born, not made! Someone with prodigious talent makes it to the top. However, staying at the top is more a matter of temperament than talent.

We all know that Virat Kohli's contribution to Indian cricket has been huge and overwhelming. From blowing kisses over an extended bat to blowing the opposition away with the wizardry of his willow, Virat has promoted a brand of leadership that is too intense to be sustainable. Leadership is about taming the galloping horse of talent with the reins of temperament. Following your passion without discrimination may land you in the mud with a thud, as many leaders have discovered. Talent may eat mediocrity for breakfast, but temperament eats talent for dinner.

Organizations feel a lot like a mixed pickle. Inside a jar of spiced oil, sweet mango and tender lime mingle freely with fiery chillies. Every organization has its own culture, shaped by hot stories, sizzling characters and floating spicy gossip. A formidable corporate mixed pickle is formed by the corporate mix of marketing, IT and HR personnel. The marketing people fill the office space with a lot of innovative energy, such as by boosting the sale of tobacco by giving away free toothpaste. What an idea!

The IT folk are more fact-driven. They are prone to the disease of narrating unpleasant and hard facts. That is why they need to be kept as far away as possible from the reception areas and customer-care centres. The HR gang brings in much-needed comic relief on a busy day, such as by chanting *Om Mani Padme Hum* before a performance appraisal. IT and HR exude a mixed taste of algorithmic and altruistic motivation. Marketing and IT bring a sweet synthesis of disparate data massaged with mustard oil. HR and marketing are an explosive combo of economic truth and extravagant lies. Leadership is the very synthesis and taste or reason of this mixed pickle. A leader is the harvester of hope in this hopeless world.

Given the hopelessness of the current world situation (pandemic, war, and looming climate catastrophe), it is time we saw some rays of hope from someplace.

Here is a poem of mine I found on my scribble pad celebrating the voice of hope:

The Voice of Hope

Soft as the quiver of a flower opening.
A flower in full bloom is hope for the bee.
Hope buzzes on the wings of aspiration.
When it aspires, the bee becomes greater than it is.
When it becomes greater than what it is,
The bee merges its sweetness into one big hive.
Hope creates a hive out of the heart of a flower.
As long as there is a flower, there is hope for the bee.

8

Unleashing Soft Power

Diversity encompasses the acknowledgement, understanding, acceptance, valuation, and celebration of differences among people concerning various aspects, such as age, class, ethnicity, gender, physical and mental abilities, race, sexual orientation, spiritual practice and public assistance status. India's soft power emanates from its rich heritage and culture. Unlike many other countries that have assimilated a more homogeneous or 'Westernized' culture, India's cultural fabric remains diverse yet cohesive, extending across the length and breadth of the nation.

Seeking coherence in the diversity around us is the essence of education.

The face of educational leadership has been changing in the twenty-first century. The new face is softer and less formal than in the previous centuries. I have tried my best to address the gender parity issue at IIMK and have endeavoured to bring much more to the system. As a strong proponent of inclusivity, I have directed all institutional efforts towards inclusion, whether it is in hiring specially-abled staff or in taking an interest in protecting the living rights of cats and dogs on campus rather than just human rights.

IIMK has been celebrating soft power over the last decade. It has played a pioneering role in making gender diversity an important component of the IIM narrative. It is a fact that, historically, many institutions, including the army, had latched on to the assumption that women can't make it there. This was an assumption based on what scholars describe as 'learned helplessness'. The soft power of women in leadership comes about not through cosmetic inclusion of them in institutions but only when women engage in the hard task of building nations and institutions. Female leaders have to embrace not just autonomy but also agency. The old boys' network can work shoulder to shoulder with the bold women's network.

Soft-power leadership is no longer about hierarchy but about 'multiarchy'. It is not so much about rigidity as it is about resilience. The soft power of flowing water will cut through the hard power of rock. According to Sandberg, Facebook's former COO, 'There will be no female leaders in the future. There would just be leaders.'

One of the seminal achievements of IIM Kozhikode has been its focus on building a new ethos around gender diversity. To nurture the cause, during my previous five-year tenure (2009–2014), the institute was credited for admitting more (than 50 per cent) women than men to its flagship post-graduate programme in 2021.

I aimed to start a movement that is irresistible and irreversible because its time had come. Then it becomes part of the system. Beyond my time, there is a reality that I cannot map, but I can do the little bit that I can. In achieving gender parity, IIMK managed to raise the ratio of women in its ranks to 54 per cent. Since the inception of the first IIM in 1964, the percentage of women at IIMs has remained in the range of 8–11 per cent. The national average of women in IIMs is now 26 per cent. Our decision to raise the number of women at IIM impacted the national average in favour of women. Six members of the board of governors at IIM Kozhikode are women. While women constitute 50 per cent of the population and the world at large, it would be a disservice to India as a modern civilized nation if one's thinking and classrooms did not reflect this. If a girl gets into an IIM from a village, she becomes a talking point there, and her son or daughter will be inspired and begin an important cycle from there.

Because of the aspirations created among women, many company boards needed female representatives but could not find suitable candidates. But how would they find them if we did not create enough space for women within the educational sphere itself? We, at IIMK, have contributed in a small way to increase gender diversity in Indian education.

Diversity is important because it brings together multiple intelligences to solve a problem. One might have what is termed 'verbal intelligence'—meaning, one can articulate one's views well. However, another individual may not possess the same quality but can be no less capable. I was invited to address students at the Oxford Said School of Business. It began raining, and I visited a grocery store near my hotel, run by an Indian, to buy an umbrella.

As I looked around, the store guy came up to me and asked, 'Sahab, kis liye aaye hain [Why have you come, sir]?' I told him the purpose of my visit, and he immediately asked, 'May I come to hear the talk? I have never met an Indian at this store who is giving a talk at Oxford.' I replied in the affirmative, but he was quick to say, 'I am uneducated.' I was taken aback, but I told him, 'No one is uneducated. You enter a customer's mind through his heart by enticing him to buy your umbrellas. I enter my customers' hearts (my students) through their heads. You move from my heart to my head. I go from head to heart. I don't possess the intelligence you do, because I can't sell like you.'

In the education space, with problems becoming more complex with each passing day, diversity is more critical than ever before.

Perhaps the male students will feel that this is tampering with what is conventionally known as meritocracy. How do we start mapping and measuring that meritocracy? Do we begin mapping it from the time the students were born? Or by mapping the atmosphere they were born into? Or from the time they graduated? Historically, if part of our population has not had the best of inputs, then their mental model would turn out to be different from that of the rest. For example, if I am often told, 'You are inferior because you are an Indian', when I go abroad, the first thought that will occur to me upon hearing this will be, 'I am amongst superiors.' I will be limited then in everything I do The same thing happens in our homes. We send subtle signals that one gender is not adequate to compete in the world, so they must be prepared to live in a less competitive world.

Assessment of merit has to be based on the difficulty level of the challenges faced. In fact, some of the female faculty at IIMK opposed the changed lenses more than the male faculty did. They felt it diluted their position because they had made it to IIM despite the odds. The odds continue to be of huge proportions. Given the daily number of female foeticide cases, being born itself is a significant achievement for an Indian female. We are merely restoring the balance.

The institute led significant changes owing to its move towards diversity. As an institution, IIMK had to pay attention to the toilets, hostels and the nature of conversations between a professor and students. The atmosphere shifts, but one sees only gradual changes in behaviour. Women's representation in the faculty, which stood at less than 5 per cent in 2009, went up to 10 to 11 per cent after my first term as director, and now it's nearly 26 per cent in 2023. And why not? One cannot imagine a country where 50 per cent of the population is female reaching its peak of economic success with half its population hidden. It's simple: when a woman is armed with an IIM degree, generations are inspired. For a man, the degree gradually stops with him.

India must recognize the importance of ensuring diversity in the classroom, not just in terms of gender but also of nationality. Diversity leads to augmented discussions with varied viewpoints, where students learn from each other, not only about different concepts but also about each other's temperaments, perspectives and personalities. In terms of raw intelligence, Indians are sharper than our Western counterparts. Pullela Gopichand, the chief national coach for the Indian national badminton team, echoes my view: 'Even if Indian badminton players achieve only 70 per cent of the physical agility of westerners, they will make up for it by superior intelligence.' Today, in the US, American students feel threatened by those from Asian countries because they feel the latter are taking away their seats in colleges. However, when it comes to challenging assumptions, asking questions and raising issues, students from the West score higher.

IIMK offers several programmes specifically designed for women entrepreneurs, managers and leaders, and many women have benefited from them. When you customize something to suit a particular demographic, it provides the necessary tools for self-belief, which I think is imperative. I believe most women operate under an invisible glass ceiling, which automatically prevents them from entering the playing field, whether in education or the corporate world. This playing field, mind you, is open to them, but they need the confidence to break through that glass, which these specialized programmes offer.

IIM Kozhikode was the first to recognize the need for different lenses when it came to female students and the need for a change in women's representation on the board. In a conference of female CEOs, I heard that behind every successful woman at work lay herself. When I was invited to speak, I just added that behind an outrageously successful woman was an astonished mother-in-law. There is research evidence that success and likeability are positively correlated in the case of men. However, for women at work, success and likeability are often negatively linked. Sheryl Kara Sandberg, chief operating officer at Facebook, pitches in support of this research: 'When men are aggressive, they are called bosses. When women are aggressive, they are called bossy,' she says.

My book, *Invincible Arjuna*, is about the making of a hero. It is also about the making of a she-ro! The need for parity is a human urge that has existed at all times in human history. In this book, there is a conversation between India's iconic warrior Arjuna and an exceptional woman, Chitrangada, whom he loves and marries. Chitrangada discovers that Arjuna is smitten by her beauty. She realizes that he is likely to either deify her or defile her in a fit of passion. So she says, 'Do not put me above yourself on a pedestal as a deity to be worshipped. Do not leave me behind in callous indifference. If you truly love me, Arjuna, keep me by your side as you walk the path of danger and daring. If you allow me to share the great dharma of your life, then you will truly know the heart of a woman.'

Many societies and organizations are caught in a dehumanizing narrative of what it means to be a woman. Women deserve the power of parity more than the cushion of charity. While women comprise almost 50 per cent of the world's population, they have just 10 per cent of the world's income and own a dismal one per cent of the world's property. The power of parity between women and men can build prosperous societies and progressive organizations. There is evidence to suggest that when men share the housework with women, their children do better in school. The success of a child in school has a positive correlation with the educational attainment of the mother. Gender parity leads to complementarity in roles. Complementarity leads to both professional success and personal fulfilment. Our workspaces must leverage the different but compatible skills that men and women bring to the table. Women can grow to their fullest potential without men having to be marginalized.

I often take photographs of the flower rangoli prepared by the staff in the reception area in front of my office and thank them personally, which motivates them. The colourful pictures of my horticulture staff's work with their exquisite beauty now appear on the walls of the campus. Every single human being around us should be treated uniquely. When I smile at the security guard, call him by his name, and ask after his family, one can see the spark in his eyes. He is touched and sometimes overwhelmed in the process.

Juhi Baruah, a former classmate and now the human resources director at Assam Don Bosco University, said: 'I know Professor Debashis Chatterjee since my student days in the post-graduate management programme. For me, Debashis stood out as the balanced factor as he was always kind and humble in all his interactions though his impressive razor-sharp intellect at times threw some of our esteemed professors off balance with his original point of view.

'And in a way, this has been so credible with Debashis that he has stood his ground, calm, dignified with logic and analysis, advocating for building institutions based on deep learning in the volatility and uncertainty of today's world. His panache for articulating his thoughts in incisive writing has contributed to the body of management knowledge and he continues to "open the door" and philosophize across platforms which is again the essence of a true educator to collaborate, build bridges, celebrate the diversity of thoughts, and unravel assumptions to ideate through myriad lenses.'

Inclusivity is visible on the IIMK campus, where all kinds of living forms co-habit. I sometimes feel that the institute and its stakeholders have encroached on the habitat of the flora and fauna of the two hills of our campus located in a pristine environment and that we human beings need to be sensitized to co-exist with the plants and animals at IIMK. This sensitivity soon gave rise to the Forum for Living Rights, which I instituted to spread awareness among the campus community about being compassionate and kind to animals, to safeguard the flora and fauna as well as ensure the safety of the campus residents. We constructed a shelter for dogs and also built small huts for housing cats.

When I hired expert faculty and staff from different backgrounds and races, I added another level of diversity to the institutes I led. Knowledge is not the right of the elite or those from urban areas. Talent may come from small towns and villages too. Life exists in multiple shades of different colours as well as in the same colours. Despite the diversity in life's manifestations, there are also common threads that unite us all. Just as colours can be shared across different objects and elements, there are universal experiences and emotions that humans share, like love, happiness, grief, and empathy. It highlights our interconnectedness and the fundamental similarities that bind us together as living beings. I have ensured inclusivity in visible and invisible, explicit and implicit, forms.

I, as a teacher, strive to energize people to embrace freedom, and I aspire to seek the truth in every problem I attempt to solve. My teachings are deeply rooted in timeless ideas, fostering resilience against intellectual coercion, and promoting openness to diverse perspectives. People should be forced to think about why they are here in a world that is obsessed with a very materialistic version of happiness. One travels from the idea of the accumulation of resources to the actualization of potential. Surya Prakash Pati, my doctoral student at IIML and now, a colleague at IIMK, once told me, 'Working with you is always a moment of truth. Nothing is small enough to escape your concern and attention.'

Shubhasis Dey, another colleague from IIMK, says, 'Professor Chatterjee's contribution to IIMK has been special. The innovative journey that he started with his path-breaking leadership in gender diversity to the launch of the post-graduate programme in liberal studies and management not only culminated in IIMK achieving its career-best NIRF MBA ranking among the top three IIMs, but also in its recognition by global peers in the form of the coveted EQUIS accreditation. The way Professor Chatterjee led IIMK with his infectious optimism, energy, authenticity, generosity, and, above all, his incredible sense of humour, is simply unmatched.'

'Beyond the influence of Prof. Chatterjee's teaching on students, I also distinctly recall an anecdote about his sense of fairness and respect,' Akhil Krishna, an IIML alumnus, reflects. 'Prof. Chatterjee once invited a renowned guest who spoke well and shared interesting thoughts. Unfortunately, he said something that inadvertently hurt a student, and she immediately raised a strong objection. Prof. Chatterjee handled the situation with great poise and moderated the discussion to ensure that an apology was tendered and that the student's pain was addressed. Prof. Chatterjee's maturity in handling the matter was instructive for all of us.'

9

Entrepreneurial Spirit and Innovative Streak

I have been described as an edupreneur by my peer group. An edupreneur is an entrepreneur in the world of education. The entrepreneurial spirit is a mindset. It is an attitude and approach to thinking that actively seeks out change rather than waiting to adapt to it. It is a mindset that embraces critical questioning, innovation, service and continuous improvement. The entrepreneurial spirit has always fascinated me and inspired me to provide a blank canvas for my faculty, staff and students, for each to paint their innovative streak, innovativeness being the very essence of entrepreneurship.

Institutions grow when they adapt to changing times. The world rallies around the evolving number of unicorns, and the generations spread across baby boomers and millennials have risen to the reality of becoming their masters. This, in turn, has provided an impetus to the entrepreneurial spirit of an already enterprising

India. The visionary endeavours of the institute's leadership blossomed in the form of the creation of new programmes and the genesis of a centre called LIVE headed by a gifted colleague Prof. Keyoor Purani and his team at IIMK. Entrepreneurship is a way of looking at things that cannot be given to someone. It can only be nurtured. The incubation centre at IIMK, called LIVE, takes on start-ups from Kerala and other states. The merit of an idea is understood only when it is presented. An idea should be honed at the nascent stage. The idea may not be fully baked, but helping students bake it is the job of institutions. I am delighted to see that the idea of LIVE was conceived by one of my colleagues, and I simply grew the vision of LIVE to include more than just a bunch of local entrepreneurs. I envisioned the global space in which to sell the idea of LIVE and advised on ways to attract funding from multiple sources rather than just one.

I enhanced its scope of operation to conduct learning programmes out of LIVE so that whenever we incubate a business or set in motion an enterprise by nurturing it, we also ensure that we capture the learnings from it and make them available to larger groups. So, essentially, we are not just incubating businesses; we are transferring the learnings from that activity to would-be entrepreneurs going forward. We started a learning programme in association with this incubator programme. I reconstituted the board of LIVE. What I did as chairperson of LIVE was to give it a more enabling environment to function by making the board a little more active so that they published what they learnt on the job. LIVE became a source for our other programmes. Our courses were bound to be a little more innovative when we create a periphery that is entrepreneurial in nature. We then bring the periphery back to the core of the institutional learning process.

IIMK was ranked No. 2 in the Atal Bihari ranking as the second-most innovative institution in the country. It has happened not just because of LIVE but because LIVE's spirit has entered the institutional DNA, and the outcome was a whole series of programmes: PhD (practice track), Executive Post Graduate Programme (EPGP), PGP in liberal studies and finance courses. As a result of all these, the whole nature of IIMK thinking became entrepreneurial.

Mainstreaming of a peripheral activity

You create a periphery and allow it to function independently of the institutional pressures, and as it blooms and blossoms a little bit, you bring back that capability to the mainstream. The institutional process is what I eventually employed so that LIVE did not become a one-man property but belonged to the institution. Entrepreneurship is the next move for young managers to move to the next level. Earlier, the social systems in India weren't conducive to entrepreneurship. But now there is little choice left but to be one. The social stigma associated with the entrepreneurial world will go away because when survival is at stake no one can sit idle.

Is it possible, one wonders, to live a life of purpose while doing business? One way to do so is to move from a self-centred universe to an eco-centred one, from ego-logy to ecology, and have a to-do list every day for how you can make someone else's life comfortable without waiting for an immediate return on your investment of time and energy. This is how both authentic leaders and entrepreneurs think. They are in the business of creating wealth, both social and financial. They believe in delayed gratification. They take their profits only after paying all the salaries. They do not take away all the profit. They plant some of the profits as seeds so that greater wealth is created. So, you can see that the thinking of an entrepreneurial leader is more purposeful than goal-oriented. This is why she succeeds overwhelmingly.

Entrepreneurs need to have what my friend Prasad Kaipa from Silicon Valley calls 'emergency-landing listening skills'. Let me explain this aircraft travel analogy. There are two kinds of listening required of flight passengers: safety-procedure listening and emergency-landing listening. In the former, the passengers are not listening at all to the cabin crew members while they describes the safety procedures. The latter occurs during instances of threats and opportunities linked to the passengers' very existence. When the pilot gives instructions for an emergency landing, the people on board will listen as their lives depend on them.

Entrepreneurs must practise emergency-landing listening because it provides opportunities for success in the face of threat or failure. More importantly, they have to understand how to process failure, because only a handful of start-ups will survive. To process failure, you need to learn from it, not just handle it. This kind of learning is called 'double-loop learning'.

When Bill Gates came to India, Kumar Mangalam Birla, who was travelling with him to the airport, asked him, 'How do you recruit at Microsoft?' Gates said, 'I ask some preliminary questions, and then I go straight into the aspect of how they would process failures.' Birla asked, 'Why do you bring [the subject of] failures into a recruitment interview?' to which Gates replied, 'Unless someone can describe a failure completely, he/she is unable to be entrepreneurial because only through processing failures can you understand the elements of success.' That is what entrepreneurs need, in addition to listening skills.

Ideas don't eventually run businesses; execution does. Of 100 efforts made, only one might succeed, but the mechanics behind that one successful idea will keep the others going. Thus, the entrepreneurs who succeed will create an aspirational space, and those that do not succeed will learn from them. This learning process is very important.

A failed business will provide you with valuable feedback, and even if you lose something because of it, you will succeed because of what you learned. All successful entrepreneurs will tell you that they have faced failure numerous times. I would like to narrate the story of the Gold Rush which took place in California a century and a half ago. A lot of gold was found at one particular location, and everyone from all walks of life, young and old, men and women, rushed to get that gold. There was one young man who was making iron shovels at the roadside. When asked why he was doing so, he replied that the people who wished to get gold would have to dig for it, and for that, they would require shovels—'These people will buy my shovels for the price of gold.'

I believe that innovation serves as a driving force that propels the institution forward, enabling it to adapt, evolve, and remain relevant in a rapidly changing world. The centres of excellence at IIMK are my humble effort to help boost innovation at our institute. The journey started with the Centre for Governance, dedicated to doing rigorous and impactful research on governance.

The vision is to use an interdisciplinary approach to solve complex policy problems and translate academic research into evidence-based governance practice. The institute's research blends inputs from cutting-edge developments in leadership, public policy, management, strategy and business. In partnership with bureaucrats, government agencies, non-government organizations, policy advocacy groups and regulatory institutions, IIMK performs robust research aimed at the sustainable transformation of governance systems in the country. Backed by multi-disciplinary expertise, the intention is the dissemination of knowledge, sharing of best practices and collaboration with counterparts across the globe to pursue excellence in the governance arena.

India has transformed in the last few decades in the context of a globalized, decentralized and liberalized world, and it now aspires to a significant jump in the level of its governance standards. Technological advancements should be complemented with the capacity-building of decision-makers and the creation of new platforms for collaborative learning. The Centre for Governance is in line with IIMK's vision to build a unique and futuristic space of global reckoning to nurture the finest management thinkers. By advancing the IIMK mission, and integrating concepts with applications and values, it contributes towards community development. It is envisaged as a reference centre to espouse governance thinking and help organizations ameliorate their governance apparatus. The centre is a gathering of thinkers, administrators, teachers and others committed to globalizing the best insights on governance for a changing world order.

Social innovation refers to the design and implementation of new solutions that imply conceptual, process, product or organizational change and ultimately aim to improve the welfare and well-being of individuals and communities. The weaving of social innovation into the fabric of management education is a novel concept. The Centre of Excellence for Social Innovation (CESI) was instituted to evolve it into a rich repository of social innovation practices in India through its research and publications. The hope is to create an international network of researchers, policymakers and practitioners to use the knowledge base of this centre to impact areas of research, teaching, training and policymaking involving social innovation. CESI also aims to sensitize graduating management students towards social innovation and the opportunities it yields, whether in corporate, government or philanthropic settings. It is committed to spearheading research and teaching that can have a social impact. Through its various impact assessment projects and programmes for women entrepreneurs, the Centre is working towards establishing itself as a national and international entity of repute.

To strengthen digital innovation and transformation in the institutional space, IIMK has established the Centre for Digital Innovation and Transformation (C-DiIT). Its objectives are to develop expertise in the emerging areas of digital technologies and their applications in organizations, government and society; to facilitate digitization and digital transformation of IIMK; and to support and empower society in the use and adoption of digital technologies.

Sustainability should be at the core of all transformation, and the world today is moving from consumption to innovation and from producing to caring. The sheer scale, scope and potential impact that India will have on twenty-first-century business make

IIMK's Vision 2047 of Globalizing Indian Thought a worthwhile aspiration. In a discussion on how IIMK is aligned with the country's Vision 2047, it was observed that climate as a probing area has not been emphasized enough. That was when IIMK launched the Centre for Climate (Climate Leadership, Internationalization, Management, Policy Advancement, Technology and Enterprise) Studies. The objective of this centre is to make meaningful contributions towards carbon neutrality. It aims at developing and offering short-term training programmes towards creating climate ambassadors; organizing climate talks addressing important climate-related issues to appropriate audiences; engaging in collaborative climate-related research projects—Lakshadweep Studies initiatives; and driving towards carbon-neutral educational campuses, for which an all-India competition is being launched called 'Solutions for a Carbon Neutral Campus (SCNS)'. The centre head, Prof. Deepak Dhayanithy, coined the acronym 'CLIMATE' (Climate Leadership, Internationalization and Management for Policy Advancement, Technology and Enterprise) as a succinct confirmation of the clarity of thought behind the centre's objectives.

Climate change is a huge problem that needs to be solved by the international community, national leaders and educational institutions. Institutes of eminence like IIM Kozhikode are at the forefront of real, workable solutions towards achieving the laudable climate goals that have been set at the international and national levels, as we have the responsibility of fulfilling society's needs and fuelling solutions to challenges. Research, technological innovation, entrepreneurship, leadership and environmental awareness will constitute the foundation on which the centre will endeavour to make meaningful contributions towards India's goals of achieving carbon neutrality by 2070, as envisioned by the prime minister of India.

Charles Chow, managing director of East-West Group, Singapore, got intrigued when I used words like 'egology' instead of 'ecology', 'work transformed' into 'workship', and phrases such as 'real power is not from the action but from interaction'. Chow served in the Singapore government, military and police and was strangely inspired by the Bhagvad Gita. I was a permanent resident of Singapore serving as a dean of S.P. Jain School of Global Management on sabbatical leave from IIM Lucknow. Chow held several conversations with me on Gita's wisdom and had this to say: 'Singapore, in particular, is still refining the nuggets of his [Chatterjee's] wisdom shared for better public policies in talent management and development. Basically, the question of whether to change or not is a more decisive one than the question of how to change. For the alteration and enrichment of human consciousness, it is vital to include wisdom that springs from the culture of one's own soil, thus unlocking the spontaneous energy of the people involved. Indeed, for every forward-looking innovation, there should be a discreet blend with the retrospective restoration of good ideas from the past. I am sure the aroma of Prof. Chatterjee's wisdom will linger on beyond Singapore and more.'

10

Gurukul of Gurus: Nature's Manuscript

Professor Rangalal Bandyopadhyay, from whom I learnt research methodology, had a peculiar habit. After each class, he tore off his class notes. When asked why, he said, 'Sticking to old notes makes me parrot passively the learning of the past. When I have to create new notes for the next class, I transform from a passive to an active learner.'

Active learning spaces are purposely transformed environments where students can enhance their creative and critical thinking abilities through engaging activities tailored to facilitate such development. Conventional classroom setups, with their fixed seating arrangements and limitations, are inadequate to meet the demands of modern teaching. These spaces lack the essential conditions required to implement pedagogical practices aimed at fostering students' problem-solving, communication, and collaboration skills.

The concept of 'Gurukul' is a speciality of the traditional, historical Indian education system. The Gurukul was a residential schooling system with origins dating back to ancient times in India. Known as a centre of learning, the Gurukul offered students space, serenity, discipline and togetherness with the guru for lifelong learning. Unfortunately, concrete structures with state-of-the-art architecture replaced Gurukuls in India after 1835. Commercial gains took the place of holistic development of the students, and moral science and ethical training became part of the syllabus.

As we progressed, we realized the futility of our efforts and started attempting to revive the Gurukul. The result was the mushrooming of educational institutions with the word Gurukul in their names. But, could we bring the environment of the Gurukul into our education? Well, that is something to ponder. Moreover, it is rare to find that environment in the progressive business schools of today. The Indian Institute of Management, Kozhikode, takes immense pride in introducing thought-provoking concepts that push learners beyond conventional methods of learning, fostering a relentless pursuit of knowledge and excellence.

I decided to create the Gurukul at IIMK as an experiment in open learning and uninhibited thinking, and I believe that this experiment in teaching students to transcend their mental boundaries will serve as an inspiration to other institutes to offer a free and holistic space for the unhindered exchange of ideas for the next generation of thought leaders. Indian education slowly moved from patronage to performance. I feel that while the right to education has become a law, the responsibility to educate has yet to become a culture. The school bag has given way to digital overload. In the education system, however, content is still king.

'Flexpertise', or teaching expertise that is flexible enough to adapt to the different learning styles of students, is the future of education. Schools of the future will look a lot less like police lockups and a lot more like conversation hubs where learning will happen through small group projects. Learning will move from painful rote memorization to the quest for creativity, problem-solving ability, higher-order thinking and the sheer joy of discovery.

The Gurukul as an Active Learning Space (ALS)

Active learning involves adopting any teaching approach that encourages active student participation, including engaging in learning tasks, reflecting on their work, and not just passively watching, listening, and taking notes. In the context of education, particularly management education, theoretical knowledge is applied to real-world problems. While pedagogies like case studies, simulations, and role-play enhance learners' information quotient, diary-writing, storytelling, and experience-sharing on both formal and informal topics contribute to the learners' appreciative quotient. Active Learning Spaces (ALS) are learning environments where the transfer and acquisition of knowledge occur in a fluid and authentic manner.

Gurukul at IIMK is a place where students learn from each other as well as from their gurus in a non-hierarchical and cosmopolitan context. They connect, collaborate and co-create through reflection and technology-enabled conversation. Nestled in the library at the institute, Gurukul is the most sought-after space on the campus for students and faculty alike. In these vibrant discussions, participants gather around on the ground and wooden seats, evoking a sense of ancient gurukul times. Lessons transform into captivating anecdotes, and learning turns into a profound experience. What emerges then is the fountain of knowledge—the nurturing of wisdom!

As a neologist, someone who loves to play with new words, I present you with one such word that is 'headucation'—education of the head that robs the joy of active learning from the students. I feel the future of education has to be re-imagined with the law as it has with lyrics, just as mathematics and magic will have to coexist as 'mathemagic'! Learning needs to be about more than just the earning and acquiring of skills—it has to be about discovery. Teachers must teach students how to break free: how to liberate the energy of the body and mind from mechanized, patterned, repetitive behaviours, like the motions of computerized robots. Indian education will be in pursuit of the lost reverence for life. And this is what happens in active learning spaces, where the mind is liberated, the body is relaxed, and the learning is subtle and involuntary.

Everyone who has spent time at the Gurukul has returned with something precious to share. One of my faculty colleagues at IIMK, who did a book-reading session around her recently published work of fiction, says, 'That's one place that generates absolute tranquilly and constructive conflicts at the same time.' The Gurukul is a place beyond work, which radiates immense calmness and positivity.

'Incredible!' Another visitor to the Gurukul exclaimed, 'It seems like I have reached another era of learning where the guru and the *shishya* are on the same plane of exchange.'

The basic design principle behind the Gurukul structure was to allow as many elements of the natural world to impact the learning process as possible. If you look at a typical classroom, the missing elements are natural sunlight, a sense of space, and greenery. Those are not part of the classroom ambience. The classroom is a typical cut-out from the colonial past and nineteenth-century education in motion.

I did not micromanage the design. I simply said I wanted vertical gardens with the grass underneath, some open space and enough sunlight. All these elements were present in the space that we got, and so it was designed largely based on the concept I had in mind. But our engineering department, and my dean, Prof. Anandakuttan Unnithan's suggestions, all contributed to it, and finally, we ended up with the structure we have.

Why is there a conversation about a Gurukul amid a management school's foundational matters, like analysis, case studies and analytical cross-sectional views of organizations? Fundamentally, we don't experience; we analyse the evidence of experience through reading case studies and balance sheets of companies. When you are in a natural ambience, you experience something larger than yourself. First, it gives you a sense of humility, which is missing otherwise. When you sit on a cushioned chair, it is as though you are already primed and hardened, as though you are occupying the decision-makers' role. The design of the chair itself gives the user assertiveness and a sense of control. The moment we move our students to the Gurukul ambience, we immediately realize that it is essentially humbling because you sit down on the ground there. The kind of dress you wear and the kind of disposition you have while you are sitting and listening to somebody or something can fill you with ego, arrogance, or indifference. But when you are grounded there comes a degree of humility.

The word 'humility' comes from 'humus', which means soil. So, you are at the ground level of experience, and you say, 'I am ready to soak it in; I am ready to grow the learning. I am fertile ground for learning, so let me be receptive to learning.' Immediately, the mood changes; the *mahaul* dictates the mood, and the mood is one of humble receptivity, and that transition happens instantly.

The first thing the students do when they come to the Gurukul is to remove their shoes outside. Wearing my shoes, I trample on this earth, as if I am a controller of its destiny. With my shoes off, I am in contact; I am with the earth rather than against it. That's the first cut. When you remove your shoes and go barefoot, you are reminded of a visit to a place of worship, where you go before a deity, essentially saying—'I am here in my natural state and please accept my homage.' When you enter, you sit down on the ground, and then you can see each other sitting in a circle, in a circular classroom. In a circle, there is no one superior or inferior; there is no hierarchy in learning; there is only reception and transmission.

We designed the Gurukul primarily as an outlier classroom to facilitate a cosy corner for intimate conversation, which lies outside the scope of day-to-day business. The word 'Gurukul' connotes a certain degree of homeliness, proximity to nature, familiarity with the teacher, learning with the teacher and the sharing of parts of each other's lives. It is a continuum of learning that goes from classrooms to lifelong learning. These are some of the enduring values of the institutions of our country, and they can be transmitted in this way. So, we thought that this could be a wonderful addition to the various designs of classrooms we have.

But this is a unique one. You will soon see that this will become one of the most photographed classrooms around. We did it on a certain impulse, but it has caught on.

I consider myself fortunate to have spearheaded numerous pioneering ventures in all the organizations I've been part of. Learning, I've come to realize, thrives in the uncharted space between formal structures. It is not something that can be strictly structured or confined. Just as communication follows a structured format, true understanding unfolds in the spaces in between. So, when you stand under a structure, you can truly grasp the essence of what that structure is trying to convey.

It is like the Zen story where the master is pointing towards the moon. His fingers are pointing towards the moon, but you don't clutch at his finger. You look at the moon that he is pointing towards. The structure of the classroom should produce a degree of understanding. Pedagogy is like a ladder; it is not the end-all and be-all. It's like a method. How do I go from this roof to that roof? I use a ladder. I use pedagogy to move from this orbit of learning to that orbit of learning. We are using these structural elements to communicate something very different from the usual way of learning. In the traditional setup, you have a fixed solution or answer that is given to you, and you analyze things to share information. But we're doing things differently.

The entire journey of education is about awakening the learner. The role of a guru is to bring clarity to the clutter of information. One meaning of the word 'guru' is 'someone who leads the student from darkness to light'. In that sense, a guru is a missionary of clarity.

11

Reaching Beyond Our Grasp: Vision 2047

A century ago, the very idea of a politically independent India did not exist. The sovereignty of kings and royalty was forged into a republic of the masses by the adoption of a Constitution only several decades ago. The road to Independence in 1947 was paved with pain, poverty and the passionate cries of our freedom fighters. Will India in 2047 be vastly different from India in 1947? Will the idea of India remain the same as our poets, politicians and trailblazers imagined it? Will there be nearly 500 million WhatsApp users in the country, the highest number in the world, shaping its mind space? Shall we tweet a new Constitution defined by a few characters? Will India's population of 1.4 billion just remain a head count, or will those heads be taken into account in shaping its national policy? Will doctors, engineers, managers and farmers turn into dreamers? Will universities be the hotbed of unicorns? Only the Republicans can answer.

Today's India is assertive. India still wakes up to the aspiration of a force for good in the world. In the year 2047, independent India will be 100 years old and IIM Kozhikode will be fifty. Will transcendental changes mark India's turning a century old in 2047? Will the new face of India be the world's topic of discussion? Will the transformation of the nation from a liberated infant to a mature, independent world power happen in the next couple of decades?

There is no guarantee that the certainties of today will hold then. We will need new ways of thinking, new skills and bold, positive imagination. IIMK has set for itself a preeminent role in 'Globalizing Indian Thought' (the institute's dictum). The potential impact that India could have on twenty-first-century businesses makes us believe that this is a legitimate aspiration. It is our earnest hope that our experiences and Vision 2047 will be of inspirational value to managers and institutions that wish to contribute to the future of India and the world. At IIMK, we wish to play our part in the creation of a new and resurgent India.

IIM Kozhikode has flourished holistically, fostering a symbiotic relationship between nature and human endeavour. The campus prides itself on meticulous attention to detail, evident through the implementation of various policies, encompassing non-smoking, waste management, and environmental preservation. Waste materials are diligently sorted into distinct categories, while smoking is strictly prohibited within the campus boundaries. Moreover, cutting down even a single tree requires prior permission of the highest authority. The horticulture staff adheres to a well-defined tree-cutting policy that aims to maintain the campus' greenery and ecological balance. Water resources are utilized with utmost care, ensuring efficient and sustainable usage. This dedicated effort has preserved the campus' pristine condition, making it an ideal model for the twenty-first century, envisioned even for the year 2047.

The role of autonomy in the future of educational practices is an important debate in our intellectual arena. After thirty-four years, India reopened this debate with its National Education Policy (NEP) in 2020, and autonomy is at the core of future educational practices.

Currently, the clamour for autonomy in educational practises is a mixed bag of pretentious idealism and hard-nosed practicality. The greatest insurance for autonomy is excellence in student outcomes rather than the piece of legislation which grants it autonomy. As long as institutions continue to excel, they will earn their autonomy through social, community and citizen sanctions. In practice, autonomy cannot be defined by entitlement or limited by unlawful encroachment. By 2047, autonomy has to be imbibed as an institutional culture rather than as a personal perquisite of a vice-chancellor, principal or director. There should be autonomy in teaching methods, autonomy of the learner in creating her curriculum, and autonomy of thought and self-governance—'*Swayttata*'.

Learning would evolve radically. In 2047, six billion people in the world would constitute the middle class. With little money but an enormous hunger for learning, they will define the learner base for a networked global university system.

The advancement of technology will permeate various aspects of intelligence, encompassing both hardware and software domains. Smart schools and smart classes may soon morph into smart chairs and smart desks. Teachers will evolve from ringmasters to Zen masters, raising awareness rather than delivering content. The four core tasks of the university—creation, dissemination, accreditation, and monetization of knowledge—will require a sweet synthesis of algorithm and altruism. Learning will involve the mobilization of knowledge for a specific person in a specific context to face specific challenges or problems. In the ultimate analysis, learning will be about the propagation of crucial questions rather than pre-determined answers. The delight and ecstasy of learning—*Ananda*—must coexist with the pressure of performance.

There would be enhanced coherence across fields. Silos will either cease to succeed or possibly disappear. Different fields will emerge stronger with coherent efforts. Transdisciplinarity will be the norm. It is about creating a coherence of intellectual frameworks beyond the disciplinary perspectives. Knowledge will move from discipline-based units to unity of meaning and understanding. The reductionist knowledge of the West, which explains the whole as the sum of its parts, will yield space to the quest for the partless whole that the rishis of the Upanishads described as '*Purnatwa*'.

I strongly believe that educational institutions will play the role of connecting hubs, largely because of technological innovation. Technology-led innovation will take learning from cognition to immersion. Traditionally, students in professional courses learn through field and factory visits. Today, it is possible for a factory experience to be simulated in a classroom. A classroom will not be a place but a space. An institution will not be just a brick-and-mortar house but a connecting hub that will digitally decode, deliver and disseminate knowledge. Disruptive innovation will enable technology to give greater access to hitherto exclusive knowledge and fulfil unmet learner needs. Technology will not be a cosmetic add-on but serve a strategic purpose. The seamless harnessing of talent and technology will come about naturally.

In general, human values tend to disappear in the face of too much technology, innovation and change. Indian teachers will be engaged in crafting global mindsets based on three classical Indian values that IIM Kozhikode has adopted for itself: *Satyam* (authenticity), *Nityam* (sustainability), and *Purnam* (wholeness).

Courses will be based on how learners receive information, not on what information they receive; they will be based on how to think rather than on what to think. Education is finally about creating and sustaining wholesome cultures rather than serving as the template for outmoded civilizations. We might have acquired the mindsets of clerks, coders and imitators to serve a civilization that bets on material values like exploitation of nature and increased consumption. While civilization is about what we acquire, culture is concerned with who we become. The most valuable outcome of education would be the development of a competent and compassionate human being. A teacher's role in India will be to mid-wife this transformative rebirth of the citizens of our great nation.

It is no secret that the business landscape of the present is in constant flux and is continually disrupted by intrinsic as well as extrinsic factors. The country is witnessing a new dawn, with paradigm shifts in business fundamentals. Sustainability will be at the core of the transformation. The three Ds—digitalization, diversification, and disruption—will redefine business shifts post-pandemic. However, it would also be naive to go for a one-size-fits-all plan. Every industry will face unique challenges and will need to renew its orientation. In any case, businesses that meet these changes with innovative thinking will have the best chance of adapting and prospering. Sustainability will be at the core of all such transformations. Capitalizing on the human element will be the key to future success. Going forward, digital education is likely to be fully integrated into mainstream education. Digital will be the nuts and bolts of learning. However, the romance of learning will still remain largely offline.

Industry engagement

The institute engages with the industry throughout the year. In a given year, the institute hosts two placement processes: the summer internship and the final placements. Other events, like leadership talks, industry conclaves, boot camps and academic workshops, are organized by various IIMK student bodies at various points in the year. The institute also facilitates live projects for its students. In addition, the students participate in numerous domestic and international competitions hosted by prominent organizations, which often result in pre-placement job offers. Over the years, the faculty members have engaged in consultancy projects and collaborated with industry on intellectual outputs, such as industry reports and white papers, which has helped strengthen our industry connection. The strong support we receive from the large and illustrious institute alumni base has been our bulwark against market cycles and shocks like the coronavirus pandemic.

Tech intensive

It is a fact that edtech companies have significantly contributed to making volumes of lessons fit right into your palm by making them accessible. They have revolutionized how the receiver chooses to receive information. However, at the end of the day, technology cannot entirely dictate the quality of educational output; it is the humans involved in the process who will complete the holistic delivery cycle. Edtech companies have realized that partnering with leading educational institutes is the way ahead for education. Will Netflix marry Harvard or will IITs and IIMs embrace Amazon or Google? That is a question for the future. Further, the unbundling of their programmes into stackable courses will help edtech promote management education by making the courses more flexible. The faculty also have constant interaction with academia, foreign universities, corporations, alumni, government agencies and research-driven assignments, which helps them be a step ahead of the game.

Disruption ahead

The education sector needed some kind of impetus to get us all to rethink how we educate and what we are preparing our students for. I saw this as an opportunity for mass experimentation in remote learning and teaching. The necessity to keep the show running eventually witnessed the deployment of digital technologies to modify, if not transform, the education sector radically into a hybrid learning mode. This mode gives us the chance to explore a sweet synthesis of the two worlds—offline and online. We have successfully integrated this into our daily functioning, keeping in mind the concerns emerging from the spread of Covid-19.

Research is one area that we need to focus on to be on par with the best business schools in the world. Factual knowledge and the intellectual infrastructure for research in leading education systems around the world are already in place in a way that they are still not in India. If we take the example of Harvard University, it is incomparable in terms of its research facilities and funds not just with Indian universities but with most universities in the world. However, in terms of the talent pool for research, India has enough resources. The only problem is that our research acumen has not been honed because we did not have a research culture in this country for a long time. In India, the building of research universities is only a recent phenomenon. However, given our New Education Policy and its thrust on research and interdisciplinary work, I do hope that our education system will soon touch a new orbit going forward.

Future forward

The future of management studies in India will be shown the right path by NEP 2020, which is a golden reset button for our education system. The next ten years will thus be crucial, as the study of liberal arts will propel the next generation of managers who will rule with their brains but also listen with their hearts. With the government's thrust on their internationalization, the IIMs will also be attracting a large number of foreign candidates into their fold. Our institute's mission of 'Globalizing Indian Thought' closely aligns with the government of India's thrust towards the same through its 'Study in India' programme. India as a global learning centre will flourish, and I hope to see IIM Kozhikode leading the charge. I also hope that the cause of gender diversity, which IIMK has been passionately promoting and propagating for the past decade, will lay the foundation for an equal and representative future for management education in our country.

12

Power of Informality

At IIMK, the relationships between the different people involved have been shaped by a bit of informality, and I feel lucky to have helped foster this informality. Informality complements the formal, like a hug after a handshake. One has often witnessed the informality of customs and costumes blur the formal lines of control (LoCs) in organizations. I saw Prof. Dipak Jain, former dean of INSEAD and the Kellogg School of Business, using the shoulder squeeze to start an informal conversation with colleagues. A spiritual guru of the masses welcomes her devotees with a lingering bear hug.

In the high-tech environments that we live in, a touch of the informal is often very refreshing, like a dash of pickle in a drab meal, although some people may find it irritating.

Establishing strong connections with the office staff is crucial. Organizations are essentially intricate webs of relationships among individuals. Sustaining these networks involves actively engaging in the art of sharing magical moments, creating an alchemy that binds people together. The foundation of shared values is more critical than the mere metrics of high performance. I find great joy in bonding not only with my colleagues but sometimes also with their families, which I affectionately term the 'Waves of Life'. This interconnectedness and camaraderie bring a deeper sense of fulfilment and meaning to my work experience.

I spent the morning of 14 November 2021, with our campus children amid a long pandemic. One sensed the energy and the enthusiasm of the wise, young kids. They knew much more than their voices could express. They expressed a lot more through their sparkling eyes and vibrant gestures than they could through words. I saw my entire life as a small wave—pretty much like an 'S' curve. One wave of life rises and subsides, making way for another. A wave carries with it the surge of the entire ocean. Those children carry with them the DNA of our entire human universe—past, present, and future—rolled into a small and glittering ripple of a human being! To quote the poet T.S. Eliot, 'For a while I was living to live in a world of time beyond me.'

Madhusoodan V., an administrative officer at IIMK, remembers his first encounter with me. He says, 'I remember our first meeting with the professor on his assumption of the office of director when he said that I will ensure the restrooms are neat and clean, the switches will work to bring light, and the taps will bring water, not air. I would like to connect this growth to glory with that humorous statement that suggested total and unconditional attention. His love for excellence and perfection is a clear-cut deviation from the evolved style of *jugaad* many are accustomed to. He pays attention to the minute aspects that would slip the attention of many others and grab the unwanted attention of others.'

Another colleague from IIMK, who did not wish to be named, recalls approaching me during the COVID-19 pandemic for help on a more personal level. 'Prof. Chatterjee took it [the problem] as his own and wanted to ensure it was done. I am forever indebted to this personal gesture. The world only checks the outcomes. How he manages some of these outcomes through people is what the world does not witness.'

I have always tried to go the extra mile to energize people to become, from who they are, to what their potential is. I empower them, thereby making them more productive and filling them with a sense of ownership. Someone needs a little help to run his home. Someone needs money to pursue a course. Another one needs just a hug. Leaders don't hesitate to help.

Neli Rasovic, a Montenegrin diplomat, remembers the conversation she had with me. At that time, Neli was in the early years of her career, investing all her time and effort in pursuit of professional success. Irrespective of the results she achieved, she always felt a lack of happiness. She says, 'So, I asked Professor Chatterjee, how can true happiness be achieved? He provided me with an enlightening answer in a very figurative way. He took out his business card and stated that it contained information about his profession. He then took an empty card in one hand and wrote down the things he really enjoyed doing in his spare time, and told me that happiness can be achieved only when a person equally integrates all the contents of his or her life, the personal and the professional. That was the moment I understood that I had to work on my personal well-being in order to better perform at my job and achieve greater results.'

Edina Avdic was selected to participate in the Indian Technical and Economic Cooperation (ITEC) programme and attended the Certificate Course in Performance Management Systems in 2018. Edina says, 'Just as light expels darkness, knowledge expels ignorance, he [I] said, with a smile on his face. Then, accompanied by the light of a peacock-shaped lamp, he started his lecture, and all of a sudden we were immersed in an unusual sea of brilliant storytelling comprising history, science, real-life experiences, relevant references and meaningful comparisons. Professor Chatterjee made our experience even more memorable by choosing to give each participant a gift: his own book with a unique hand-written inscription dedicated to us. The depth of his understanding of human nature creates a dwelling for him in the heart of every person he meets.'

Jayant Pawania, who graduated from IIM Lucknow and is now, a senior leader in the banking industry, says: 'Prof. Deb Chat was always a visionary; he never thought or spoke short-term. He would tell us to become good leaders and not just good managers and would articulate it very beautifully by saying, "Please do not confuse leadership with the dealership." A kind and compassionate person, he made it a point to visit the placement waiting halls. He would talk to students, especially the anxious ones. While I was having a little bit of a hard time during placements, he came around, inquired about my interviews and told me to not worry and keep trying; if by chance things did not work out by the evening, I could go straight to his office, and he would take care of things. I spent five minutes with him, and with the positive energy he infused in me, I met him in the evening with good news. As a renowned scholar and professor of leadership, Prof. Deb Chat has been able to find the connections as well as the disconnections between ancient Indian wisdom and modern management theory and practices. He would often lament the unfolding crisis of lack of leadership across the world and how it is wreaking havoc on the planet, corporations and humanity as a whole. His recent work is an earnest attempt to bring these challenges and opportunities therein to the fore.'

Kushal Raj Chakravorty, another alumnus of IIM Lucknow and now, the founder of Lotus Petal Foundation, says that he owes his vocation of giving back to society to what I once said: '"Stepping out of this campus, with this education, you can either decide to be a mercenary or a missionary." As the words washed over me, I believe it was that day that the seeds for my eventual move from the corporate world to the arena of social service were sown.' Kushal and his partner Saloni run a free school for the children of migrant labourers in Gurgaon.

Vartika Dutta, faculty, IIM Amritsar, says, 'Prof. Chatterjee is a real guru who, as a custodian of values, asks you the right questions so that you can seek the answers yourself by choosing a path that might not always be an easy one. Because of him and his contribution to the field of educational leadership, I feel compelled to go above and beyond to develop passionate, value-driven, transformational educators.' Pronobesh Banerjee, a colleague at IIMK, asserts that, 'apart from his laser focus at a professional level, what has touched me deeply is Debashis' compassion for faculties, which I have witnessed at a personal level. I remember when I went through several personal crises, Debashis' compassion was a strength that helped me to remain afloat.'

Prof. Asha Bhandarker, another colleague and well-known academic from IMI, Delhi, observes, 'Debashis is a genial-looking professor with a smile on his face, a positive attitude, and one who oozes humanity through his demeanour. His kind and informal personality brings forth a profound sensation of calm in everyone around him. He has also been highly aware of his persona and has cultivated it well—something that more directors ought to do. Many directors are not very self-aware, and this does affect their public image. He has the strong aspiration to take Indian wisdom globally.'

The Managing Director of SDA Bocconi Asia Centre, Alessandro Giuliani, says of me, 'Whenever I met him, whether at 7 a.m. between flights or at IIMK, it was a great experience on a personal, intellectual, and academic level each time. At a personal level, his empathy and personalized remarks, as well as his diverse perspectives, have helped me understand different facets of Indian thought. At an intellectual level, his deep understanding of ancient texts and the breadth of their relevance has given me a whole list of insights on how to capture the complexity of Indian minds and behaviours and their roots. Academically, I have always been impressed by his visionary approach to business education, with an eye on new practices and needs and on anchoring them and giving them meaning through well-rooted traditions.'

Rajeev Kumra, professor and former dean from IIM Lucknow, describes my leadership style as 'people-oriented'. He goes on to say 'He has the quality to identify the good qualities of his teammates. He is also kind enough to give credit to his teammates in public for what they have done. His colleagues have approached him in their good and bad times for guidance.'

Dr Kiran Bedi proudly adds, 'I have learned a lot from every interaction with him. Prof. Chatterjee, while speaking at length about purpose, productivity and possibilities at Raj Nivas, won our hearts and punctured many illusions about leadership. Prof. Chatterjee's sense of wordplay and his observations on the minute things around us are a class apart. He astutely assimilates Indian thought into Western management practices. He is a wordsmith. I have always valued him for his understanding of varied subjects, from history to literature to management to spirituality. He is a friend who shares objective advice. Whenever I have visited IIM at his invitation, I have enjoyed every moment spent on the campus, which is the epitome of his nobility. He is a very simple person who relishes every moment of his life and who finds happiness within.'

Rola Ezzedine, creative director, Maison Rola Ezzedine, and founder of the Luxury of Love platform, recalls her meeting with me: 'I lived between Beirut and Paris, and when I was on business in Kuala Lumpur in October 2009, Prof. Debashis Chatterjee was one of the well-known speakers at the Asia Pacific Frost and Sullivan Global Congress on Growth and Leadership at the JW Marriott Hotel. What a coincidence! Naturally, my first reaction was to tell him how this large mind, which can go beyond the normal thinking that we usually know, can be so young! No way! Are you Deb Chat? He just laughed. A wealth of learning, acquired throughout these years of friendship! He taught me how to remove my ego, especially in my sector of business, which was surrounded by it! To take my leadership skills to a more conscious level of thinking, and how to move with confidence in a crisis situation are his enduring gifts to my professional life.'

K. Sadanandan, who was my co-worker for several years, says, 'The name Debashis Chatterjee is enough to inspire, motivate and encourage anybody in our circle. His mere presence is enough to inspire dynamism and inspire the team. One thing I noticed in all his endeavours is that he wins people over through a particular thought process. Eventually, things happen when people are convinced that something has to be done. His leadership and the kind of wisdom he possesses always make a difference in teamwork. From personal to professional aspects, I have learned so much from him and am still doing so. I believe that if there is light at the end of a tunnel in higher education, it is only because there is a teacher and leader like Prof. Chatterjee.'

Sojan George, senior executive secretary, who has been working closely with me for the last several years, says: 'He is a true legend and an awe-inspiring leader. This privileged opportunity under his leadership moulded me into someone with valuable skills and talents. Prof. Chatterjee truly elevates the workspace and the whole work experience with his electric persona and leads by example. His guidance and support have been instrumental in helping me achieve phenomenal personal and professional growth. Prof. Chatterjee, without even batting an eyelid, has encouraged so many of us in the office to strive to do our jobs better by coming together as a team and achieving the organization's goals. With his perseverance and fortitude, he has inspired us all to take pride in our work.'

'He is highly articulate and knowledgeable in a great many areas, and his easy-going conversation skills and quick wit endear him to all who meet him, and he commands the admiration of friends and colleagues,' says Dr Vyasa Krishna Burugupalli, another colleague who now lives in Kampala, Uganda. 'He enjoys teaching young students and being in their company. The students' relevant and, at times, irrelevant (at the time) questions keep their minds young, fresh and inquisitive. This was his mantra for success. Though he is the director, I am sure he prefers to be regarded as a teacher rather than as an executive. When I sought advice for my son, he immediately advised us on our next steps. It helped my son succeed in life because he followed the advice.'

Venkataraman S., Chairperson, IIMK Kochi Campus and a former CEO, says, 'Deb Chat is someone I have come to respect and admire right from the first time I interacted with him privately, and this admiration has grown over time. Right away, he struck me as someone who has the quality of being able to seamlessly blend perspicacity and action orientation. For all of his generally amicable demeanour and the endearing philosophical wisdom that he espouses with consummate ease when it comes to actions and decisions when it comes to leading, he gives you ample freedom to act, guides with gentle pointers from time to time and supervises with a light hand but expects you to take charge while conforming to the higher standards of governance.'

In my eventful three-decade-long career, I've come to realize that informal learning is like a persistent swarm of passengers surrounding a commuter train at a jam-packed Mumbai station. You step onto the train, and you're in the formal space of a passenger, with the driver following a strict, formal route to your destination. But life, as it often does, throws curveballs at you. The train might break down, meet with an accident, or get delayed indefinitely. And just like that, you find yourself exploring the many informal ways to reach your intended goal. You can hop into a cab, hitch a ride with a friend, or even take a stroll at your own pace, wherever your heart desires.

Learning institutions, like seasoned travellers, need to master the art of harnessing the space of informality, especially in challenging times. It's the ability to think outside the formal boxes and adapt to the unpredictable twists and turns that will lead them towards progress.

And let me tell you, my readers, if there's one thing I've learned from my encounters with distinguished Presidents of India, it's that embracing informality can work wonders even in the most formal settings.

So picture this: I found myself in the hallowed halls of Vigyan Bhavan, Delhi, where the inimitable Dr Abdul Kalam, the 11th President of India, was gracing the occasion with his presence. He was busy handing out awards on behalf of IIM Lucknow to eminent Indians, including the likes of Ratan Tata, Raghunath Anant Mashelkar and Ela Bhat. Now, I was a small fry coordinating the whole show along with my team of faculty at IIM Lucknow. But when the award ceremony ended, and Kalam was about to make his exit, my faculty got all starry-eyed and desperate for a photo op with the man himself.

But wait! The security guards were tough bouncers, forming a human fortress around the President. They wouldn't even hear our plea. And just when we thought we were stuck in the no-photo zone, I had an outrageous idea. I mean, what's life without a little audacity, right? So, in the presence of the great Kalam, I cried out loud, 'President, how about a photo opportunity with IIM faculty?' Oh, the gasps and stares from security were something to watch.

But guess what? Dr Kalam, bless his soul, turned around, spotted us, and without a care in the world, he jumped the rope meant to keep mere mortals like us away and stood proudly with us for that priceless photo op. Ladies and gentlemen, that was the mark of a true people's President.

Then there was my encounter with President Pranab Mukherjee, the 13th President of India, back in 2008. I had to invite him to the Institute's Convocation, and naturally, I addressed him with all due formality, as 'Mr President.' But this man, this humble soul, didn't let titles and positions define him. "Call me Citizen Pranab," he interrupted me, breaking the ice with a warm handshake and common touch that's all too rare in the corridors of power.

And finally, President Ram Nath Kovind, the 14th President of India, graced our campus alongside his better half, ready to address the Indian Management Conclave we were co-hosting with MBA Universe. As speaker after speaker fawned over him, the President shot me a cheeky glance and asked, "Do you think they'll let me speak too?" Oh, the irony! Because, my dear readers, he was the keynote speaker—the man of the hour!

Ah, the tales I could weave from these encounters! The world of formalities may reign supreme, but it's the informal moments, the candid exchanges, and the genuine human connections that truly make life memorable. Here's to embracing informality, even when the train of life gets a little bumpy, and enjoying the ride to wherever it takes us! Cheers!

Epilogue

Decoding the Mystery of the Prime Mover

Ram Kakani, a formidable professor of finance and now the director of IIM Raipur, chronicles his memory of our journey together:

> Prof. Debashis Chatterjee (Dada) has been a wonderful colleague, mentor and go-to friend for me since 2006. For me, personally and professionally, he is much more than just the director of the IIM Kozhikode. From our Singapore days to those in Dubai to the lovely conversations we had in Dehradun, XLRI Jamshedpur and of course Kozhikode, he has always had a calming influence on me. Debashis cannot just be described as a teacher par excellence in the subject of organization behaviour. You cannot define him fully by his

academic brilliance or his astute administrative skills either. I am indeed privileged to be able to share this impactful incident: It was 2007 and I was going through a crucial experience of extreme stress in Singapore. The way in which Dada and Aditi Madam helped me overcome that period of personal gloom was simply overwhelming. Those days will be etched deeply in my memory.

I am often humbled and surprised by the way people perceive my contributions to education. Some consider me as one of those teachers who made a positive impact on their lives. Over the years, I have had the privilege of writing numerous books and publications aimed at assisting readers in discovering their paths to learning. I hope that I can offer some guidance to aspiring industry leaders, professionals and entrepreneurs, helping them assess and embrace their unique strengths and values while fulfilling their individual calling (*svadharma*). My ultimate goal is to contribute to the growth of these leaders, enabling them to serve society and the environment at both local and global levels more effectively.

The Prime Mover who runs my life remains a mystery to me as I have interwoven the rough and smooth experiences into the fabric of my life. The mystery of the Prime Mover of our universe reveals itself when we learn to be authentic and unpretentious. I accept that one should live up to one's full potential by reducing internal conflicts. The only thing blocking your God-given potential is your divided mind. There are many mutinies inside your mind, but you can resolve your internal conflicts by simply observing them. The shadow of conflict ceases when the light of pure observation falls on them. I live by this life rule: the small 'p' is performance, the capital 'P' is potential, and the small 'i' is internal conflict. Your performance (p) will equal your potential (P) if you simply reduce your internal conflicts (i): p = P-i.

I am filled with immense joy knowing that I might have played a part in influencing someone like Annamia van den Heever's leadership journey over the past two decades as a development coach in far-off Africa.

Here is what Annamia had to say:

The teaching of Debashis Chatterjee has had a major influence on my own leadership career over two decades. I was introduced to his academic work when he lectured to us in a master's programme at the Leadership School at the University of KwaZulu Natal in South Africa at the start of this century. As a lecturer, Debashis was unlike any other, combining academic teaching with empathy and depth of feeling. His work introduced new areas of thinking about the importance of human values in transformational leadership from an Indian perspective. This academic programme was greatly enriched by the life-changing experience Debashis offered a group of us at the Indian Institute of Management in Lucknow in February 2002, followed by a retreat in Rishikesh in the foothills of the Himalayas. As South Africans, we were fortunate to have had Nelson Mandela as a role model. Debashis's teaching helped us make sense of the importance of how the integrity of such a leader was essential to human progress. At this retreat, on the banks of the Ganges, he guided us in real life how to see beyond what is visible and to listen beyond what we can hear. These lessons of sensing deeper into what is obvious have been with me for the rest of my career as a leader. Professor Chatterjee's work is more relevant than ever as, internationally, we face the awful reality of corruption and incompetence. May it continue and grow in years to come.

It was truly startling to witness the impact my teaching had on her and the other participants. I am sincerely grateful for the opportunity to have been a positive influence in the lives of high, potentials. Moments like these reaffirm my commitment to share my knowledge and insights for the betterment of those I have the privilege to connect with.

I am someone who believes in nurturing the heart. I always keep in mind the Japanese saying, 'Keep a green tree in your heart, and the birds will automatically come.' I believe that decoding human nature is the most important thing for a leader to do. It is only a human being, not a frog, that can think smart but act dumb. I understand that inside a beautiful face, there may lurk a mischief-maker and that, in every submissive bow of the head potentially hides a tyrant. Human beings are prone to change themselves to suit their circumstances. Change is an integral part of human nature, and I firmly believe that as leaders, we must be prepared to anticipate and adapt to these changes. Staying ahead of the game is essential, as failing to do so would limit our effectiveness and render us as futile as a chimpanzee attempting to climb a greased pole.

To me, turning a transaction into a meaningful connection revolves around paying attention to body language and putting the interests of others ahead of our own. Engaging in reciprocal disclosure fosters energetic connections, making people feel trusted, seen, heard and accepted for who they are.

Epilogue

I enjoy sharing life lessons sometimes in a light-hearted manner with such expressions in my class:

Do not walk alone; carry your environment (mahaul) with you.
Do not underestimate your strength. That is your boss's job.
You are a dignified human, not a Mickey Mouse.

In Hindi, the word *mahaul* represents the psycho-social environment that a leader carries with her. Your body is not a statue; it is a dance of energy. The body is made up of a million pulsations that create its magnetic field, influencing other bodies and the larger environment. Look into the mirror. Make your eyes kinder and gentler when you are not in hunting mode so that your gaze includes rather than isolates people. There is a certain glow that transmits through your eyes, speaks through your voice and fills your *mahaul* with subtle vibrations that will draw people to you as you walk along.

Look to something greater than yourself. Your self is more than your body's bone-and-muscle fortress. In any case, the fortress-like body is moving closer to the crematorium or burial ground each year. This is a simple rule of nature: when a bird is young, it eats worms; when the bird is dead, it is eaten by worms! Life is eternal. Death is just a change of circumstances. Mother Nature has no interest in preserving your body or even your mind forever. Dream before you die. Our everyday life is a waking dream. Your body and mind, your prized assets, are actors in a dream sequence. You can take good care of your assets for as long as possible. Your assets are not you. Assets depreciate. But the 'I' who owns the assets can only appreciate them if you allow it to.

You become wealthy not because of what you have but because of who you are. That entity called 'you' is a code word for who you really are. The 'I' is your ever-expanding identity, which can encompass an entire universe linked in a web of love. If you ask me, I would rather lie down and live in the hearts and minds of many people that I have touched than in the crematorium. 'Love something greater than yourself.' That's the only way to resurrect that interminable life that is you.

I have kept my cool while arguing for the creation of institutions based on deep learning. In the world we live in now, which is a world full of change and uncertainty, we indeed require such institutions. I employ my ability to concisely express my ideas in writing, which has added to the existing body of knowledge on management and leadership, and I will continue to ponder on matters in a transparent manner across platforms, which is again the core of a true academic—to work collaboratively, forge connections, celebrate differences in viewpoints and dispel presumptions in order to generate ideas from a variety of perspectives.

I believe that time recycles itself. Life lingers on, from the twinkle in my eyes to the wrinkle on my forehead. The only way to do something is, well, by doing it. I learned to twist an ankle by twisting it, to dance by dancing and to walk by walking. Ideas are like silent engines; they have no power by themselves. They gain power when I use my muscles and my mind to jump-start them. I have often wondered what makes me what I am and how I should describe myself—as a leader, a colleague, the head of the institution, a collection of atoms held together by an invisible power or anything else.

Often, people have complimented me for having an intuitive capacity to recognize people's capabilities and cultivate them in a variety of ways. As the director of an educational institution, I always instil the utmost faith and confidence in individuals while assisting them in defining their vision for their lives. More importantly, they have my support and guidance in charting their careers within the institution. Amidst a rapidly changing environment, I believe academic leaders have the responsibility to provide direction and order, and pursue deeper endeavours.

One lives one's natural and spontaneous self. The analogy that comes to mind is that of a river: free-flowing and flexible. This helps me deal with obstacles along the way as a river does. I am all that is reflected in the minds of my friends, colleagues and family. I am more than the sum of my parts. I am a queer synthesis of a multitude of people. I am like that river that takes on the slant of the sun and the lay of the riverbed. As a Greek philosopher has said, 'You can't step twice in the same river.' Such is life. For me, life is an evolution of our capacity to grow in awareness of who we really are on this spaceship called Planet Earth.

On the subject of a lifeline beyond one's own life, I would let my son Siddharth, who recently graduated from the Yale-NUS college, have the last words:

Asking a son to speak about his father is like asking a fish to speak about the lake it has grown up in. In one sense, there is too much to tell; in another, not much to be said at all. I have never met anyone who thinks as big as my father. This quality of his has probably defined my life in more ways than I know. I have also never met anyone who has given himself so deeply—

Epilogue

in spirit and body and mind—to the work they've felt called
to do. I am lucky that Debashis Chatterjee has been so prolific
in his life. Because I get to find a little bit of him in each of
his contributions to IIM Kozhikode, in his books and in the
people he has helped. Thank you.

References for Recommended Reading

Alvesson, M. (1995). *Management of Knowledge-intensive Companies.* Walter De Gruyter, Berlin.

Bryman, A. (2007). Effective leadership in higher education: a literature review. *Studies in Higher Education,* 32(6), 693–710.

Collins JC, Porras JI. (1996). Building your company's vision. *Harvard Business Review,* 74(5), 65–77.

Collins JC, Porras JI. (2002). *Built to Last Successful Habits of Visionary Companies.* New York, NY: Harper Collins Publishers Inc.

Esty, Katharine, Richard Griffin, and Marcie Schorr-Hirsh (1995). *Workplace diversity. A manager's guide to solving problems and turning diversity into a competitive advantage.* Avon, MA: Adams Media Corporation.

Fraguiero, F. and Thomas, H. (2011). *Strategic Leadership in the Business School: Keeping One Step Ahead.* Cambridge University Press, Cambridge.

Goleman, D. (2006). *Emotional Intelligence*. Bantam Books, New York, NY.

Kets de Vries, M. (2006). *The Leadership Mystique*. Pearson, London.

Larwood, L., Falke, C. M., Kriger, M. P., & Miesing, P. (1995). Structure and meaning of organizational vision. *Academy of Management Journal,* 38(3), 740–769.

Lorange, P. (2010). *Leading in Turbulent Times: Lessons Learnt and Implications for the Future.* Emerald Group Publishing, Bingley.

Mintzberg, H. (1998). Covert leadership: notes on managing professionals. *Harvard Business Review, 76(6),* 140–147.

Paul Baepler , D. Christopher Brooks , J. D. Walker (2014). *Active Learning Spaces: New Directions for Teaching and Learning.* Number 137 (J–B TL Single Issue Teaching and Learning), Jossey Bass Publishers.

Senge, P.M. (1990). *The Fifth Discipline – The Art & Practice of a Learning Organization.* New York: Doubleday.

Sun, M., & Chiang, F.-K. (2015). Book review: Active Learning Spaces: New Directions for Teaching and Learning (Author: Paul Baepler et al.). *Educational Technology & Society,* 18 (2), 394–396.

Thomas, H. and Thomas, L. (2011). Perspectives on leadership in business schools. *Journal of Management Development, 30(5),* 526–540.

Yukl, G.A. (1998). *Leadership in Organizations* (4th ed). Prentice-Hall, London.

Acknowledgements

The title of this book came from Manisha Mathews, former executive editor of Sage Publications. The book finally came into being because of Radhika Marwah, a brilliant and enterprising executive editor of Penguin Random House India. To both of you, I owe a debt of gratitude.

One was humbled to see that it took a large number of people to stitch together what you now see as a chronicle. I would like to acknowledge the efforts of Deepa Sethi, professor and dean of programmes and international relations at IIM Kozhikode, for painstakingly inviting the contributors and creating the first skeletal structure of the book with some help from me—I am grateful to her. I thank my research associate, Anandha Lekshmi Nair, for meticulously editing the book multiple times. I also extend my heartfelt appreciation to Kripa Raman, Yash Daiv and Penguin Random House India for their editing and constructive feedback. I am immensely thankful to all the contributors for their time and efforts towards the completion of this book. Their involvement has been spontaneous and selfless. Finally, my heartfelt thanks to my colleagues, friends, family, scholars and students, as they are all integral to the chronicle of my journey.

Scan QR code to access the
Penguin Random House India website